Ken Jones is from Shropshire. He is a former soldier who served with the Parachute Regiment, Royal Marine Commandos and various elements of UK Special Forces. Ken is the founder of Avalanche Endurance Events and Race Director of The Fan Dance Race Series Special Forces challenge. He is also a motivational speaker, an avid outdoorsman, mountaineer, competitive road cycle racer and keen chess player. Ken lives between Lucca, Italy, San Diego, California and the Elan Valley, Wales.

'Riveting. Knife-edge suspenseful. Uplifting beyond measure. Takes the spirit of Special Forces soldiering to new levels – showing how those who dare can survive the seemingly un-survivable in one of the toughest environments on earth'
Damien Lewis

'While the content is gripping, it is Jones's humour that make the story so readable'   *Daily Telegraph*

'Engulfed in a torrent of deadly snow – twice. Forced to crawl for three days through mountain gullies and icy streams with horrific injuries. And then his problems REALLY began . . . One man's riveting tale of indefatigable courage in the face of appalling odds'   *Mail on Sunday*

DARKNESS DESCENDING

KEN JONES

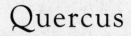

First published in Great Britain in 2014 by Quercus Editions Ltd

This edition published in 2014 by

Quercus Editions Ltd
55 Baker Street
Seventh Floor, South Block
London
W1U 8EW

All photographs supplied courtesy of the author except
p2 *Top* © Beriliu/Dreamstime.com
p2 *Bottom* © Ovidiu Iordache/Dreamstime.com

A CIP catalogue record for this book is available
from the British Library

PB ISBN 978 1 78206 602 6
EBOOK ISBN 978 1 78206 601 9

10 9 8 7 6 5 4 3 2

Text and plates designed and typeset by Ellipsis Digital Ltd

Map © Jamie Whyte

To those who never made it home.

If you ask an alpinist why he climbs mountains he'll reply: 'Because it's there.' As far as I know, no one has ever pointed out what nonsense that is. The alpinist's will isn't prompted by the mountain, it's there even without the mountain. The alpinist's will is not so petty that it needs something as random as the shape of the earth's crust in order to exist. Even if the earth was as flat as a billiard table, there would still be alpinists: the true alpinists. The true alpinist would actually be ashamed to have his will moulded by things of an order as low as mountains. So the only question that could rightly be asked of the true alpinist: why do you never climb mountains?

The Rider, Tim Krabbe

CONTENTS

PART ONE

PART TWO

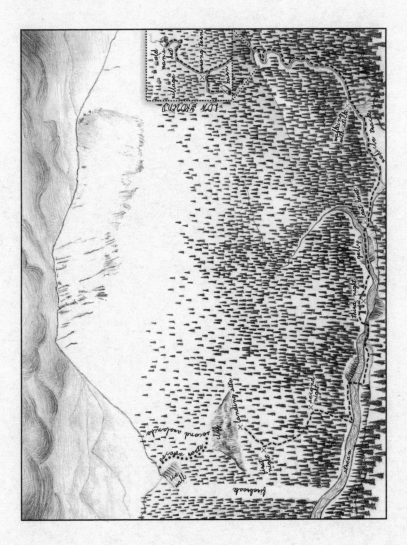

INTRODUCTION

AVALANCHE

I reached the ice wall in well under an hour, and, even though most of the work had been done by sliding on my ass, I was exhausted. The day was drawing to a close, and in 90 minutes it would be dark. Despite my scare earlier that afternoon I decided I would try for the summit again the next day and set off a few hours before first light. The slopes would freeze over with the cold of the night and the going would be firmer. I got back to my feet and walked steadily downwards. My plan was to drop a couple of hundred metres in height and find a safe place to bivi under the shelter of the trees, a good distance away from any spill channelled into the firebreak. More than anything now I was looking forward to the warmth of my sleeping bag and a hot cup of tea.

Even though I loved the feeling of metal going into ice, I lacked the energy and concentration to put my crampons back on so decided to hug the tree line and go round the sides of the ice wall where I wouldn't need them. Just as I was backing up on all fours to lower myself off a boulder, there was a distinct crack from high above me. The sound was sharp, crisp and sudden, its echo travelling downwards and flooding the open slope with a low-pitched groan. After a moment of perfect silence came a second jolt. My heart stopped, and for a few seconds I was rendered incapable of doing anything.

Avalanche!

A large part of the snow-covered ridge nearly 50 metres wide fractured in a crown shape about 500 metres above me, causing a section of the mountain to seemingly detach itself, cutting out a jagged line across the slope. At first, it slid away neatly, its motion almost uniform, then as it gathered energy and momentum, it hurtled down towards me with increased speed, churning up the smooth slopes and spitting out snow with such a force that it blocked out the sky with a white mist. It came down faster than I could have imagined, the noise and tremor was everywhere and right on top of me all at the same time. My normally wide and vigilant sense of awareness was suddenly constricted to a narrow, singular sensation of terror. I stood stupefied and unmoving, staring open mouthed like an imbecile, totally unable to remove my eyes and turn my body away from the scene that was unfolding. I was experiencing a moment of pure naked fear, of an intensity far beyond anything I knew.

PART ONE

There are moments in difficult situations, far away, that there is no more doubt. There, the questions are gone. And I think these are the important moments. If the question is gone, I have not to answer. Myself living, I am the answer.

Reinhold Messner

CHAPTER ONE

FROM THE SMOKE TO THE SNOW

Elvis Hostel – The Day Before . . .

With all my kit waterproofed and spread across the dormitory floor, I began packing it into a large canoe sack, making sure that the items I'd need most frequently were near the top: sleeping and bivi bag, poncho with bungee cords attached, long johns and sweatshirt, spare socks and gloves. Next, two broken down 24-hour ration packs stuffed into two mess tins, a gas stove and a hexamine stove with windproof matches and tablets inside, followed by a set of army issue DPM Gore-Tex jacket and trousers. At the top of my Bergen, I crammed in a smaller canoe sack which held nothing more than spare socks, a flask and a bottle of water. Inside the top flap interior compartment I kept a spare Maglite torch, a second disposable camera and a small first aid and wash kit. The outside zip pouch at the back held a full water bottle, and strapped onto the sides were an ice axe and crampons. Essential utility items, like my Leatherman tool and Silva compass were tied into my jacket pockets. I had decided to leave my GPS, satellite phone and rescue flares under my bed in Manchester. I had brought my cell phone but hadn't even turned it on. I knew there was no chance of it working in the mountains, and besides, I didn't want technological support: the essence of my plan was to disconnect to connect.

Long before I'd arrived in Romania my central plan had been to make my way out to the Fagaras range and climb Mount Moldoveanu, at over 2,500 metres, it was the country's highest peak. This part of the Transylvanian Alps was wild and remote, and although dwarfed in height by the main European Alps, the area was far less trodden by alpinists and ascents of the peaks in the winter months were few and far between. This was to be my big challenge, the means to test myself in a way that revived the sense of adventure I had missed since leaving the army. As with any new climb, there was doubt: I was going alone and knew the conditions would be harsh. I knew from the start that climbing skills here would be less important than the capacity to endure what-ever challenges the mountain might throw at me. But despite the risks of going solo, climbing in the Fagaras would bring everything I was looking for at this time in my life: self-reliance, meaning, physical challenge, escape from routine and contact with nature and its beauty. Above all, I wanted to be out in the world, breaking my own trails.

Setting Off . . .

The morning air cut into me as I paced up and down the length of the platform of Brasov train station trying to keep warm. Falling snowflakes swarmed like bees around the small balls of yellow light emitted by the station lamps. Outside the electric glow they were invisible, their cold touch on my face the only sign of their existence. I stared down at the tracks that were glazed with frost and thought how cold and hard everything looked. The day was like lead.

I began to wonder why I wasn't still in bed as my mind posted warm images of friends back home sitting cosily around the fireplace of some quaint village pub as they celebrated the New Year. Then I thought of all the other backpackers at the hostel, probably still sound asleep under their duvets. I knew that in a few hours they'd be emerging from their beds for brunch before hitting the ski slopes. Later they'd be eating out together before a night of partying in the old-town bars. In these moments I felt alone, it was something entirely different to true loneliness, but still a strong enough feeling for me to miss my friends and the festive cheer of back home. Although

I was never usually troubled by lack of companionship, there were moments when travelling that I got caught on my own. It was one of the drawbacks of travelling by yourself, those infrequent moments of separation and lack of contact. You can't just manufacture friendship or a bond out of thin air: it's something that comes naturally and often by chance, so until the world sees fit, you just have to settle for your own company. Those who have exposed themselves to the sheer uncertainty of solo travel will understand: sometimes it's all worth it, at others you wonder what on earth you're doing.

I knew that in many ways I was missing out. Although I did sometimes think about embarking on a more normal way of life, it never quite seemed to happen. Instead I was always in the midst of a challenge or planning my next adventure. I'd lost count of the times I had walked past bar windows and been called in by friends out having a good time. Too often I had to make my excuses and walk on because I was in the middle of some training regime. It could be a frustrating and solitary existence, yet there was always that moment when I knew it had all been worth it. The training would pay off and I would be able to enjoy rare and privileged freedoms. I had an adventurous and unconventional spirit and such a way of life was in my nature. After all I had experienced, I still held the philosophy that real adventure was made up of more than distant lands and mountain tops, rather it lay in one's readiness to exchange the comforts of domestic certainty for an uncertain resting place and the constant surprises that a restless life brought in its train.

Watching the countryside rolling by from the train window, my feelings shifted from melancholy to a kind of contentment. Moments like this, far away from everyone and everything, gave me the rare opportunity to take stock and reflect upon the hectic and non-stop adventures of the last few years. Life had been eventful. I had served nearly four years as a Paratrooper followed by two years as a Special Forces soldier. Now, at twenty-six, I was living a different kind of life as a student studying politics at Manchester University. My new lifestyle was challenging and a world away from anything I had previously known. I was older than my fellow students and certainly felt different, even out of place to some extent. But I'd ended up being in my element, I made new friends, the sort I would otherwise never have met, I enjoyed my classes and had plenty of time to go travelling and off on adventures.

As I considered the events that had got me where I was today, it occurred to me for the first time how fateful one moment of indiscipline had been in directing the course of my life and pushing me away from the military and back to education. As a young boy I'd been fascinated by all things army and spent many a weekend dressed in camouflage fatigues trespassing and sneaking around in the nearby military training area with my brother and some of our more unruly friends from the nearby village. As my interest grew, I would look through my dad's old books and stare in awe at worn black and white photographs of soldiers on SAS 'Selection', marching over the misty and snowy summits of the Brecon Beacons, rifles in hand and heavy-looking packs on their back. I'd been fascinated by the ability of its members to operate in any environment and had been massively impressed by stories of their legendary fitness capabilities, men who would think nothing of running 20 miles with a backpack full of bricks.

Aside from my soldierly ambitions I was a keen sportsman. The headmaster of my primary school was a former RAF officer who put a strong emphasis on sports and games, so from an early age I was always drawn towards keeping fit and an outdoor life. Growing up in the Shropshire countryside gave me a strong taste for forests, mountains and the possibilities they held for a young boy with adventure and mischief in his blood. As I got older my interest in the army was diverted, but following disastrous A-level results that left me with no chance of gaining entry into a decent university, my ideas and ambitions for a military career were revived. I'd seen TV documentaries on the Parachute Regiment and Royal Marine Commandos and knew that they were regarded as having the toughest entry requirements and being among the best fighting units in the world. I applied for both at the same time and joined the Paras as they offered the earliest opportunity to commence basic recruit training. My time as a Paratrooper was some of the best and worst in my life, and although it was something I was extremely proud of, after serving out my minimum engagement I signed off with the intention of fulfilling my ambition of attempting the Special Forces Selection course, albeit through somewhat unusual channels.

After passing Selection I served for two years, spending some time with the reserves and also the SBS (Special Boat Service). This part of my military career was without doubt the most enjoyable and satisfying and I grew both as a person and a soldier. It was there I gained skills and met friends that would have a lasting influence on the next phase of my life and who would inspire me to believe that attending university and maintaining links with the military at the same time were possible. At my first interview at Sterling Lines, the old SAS base in Hereford, the OC (Officer Commanding) asked me if I'd ever considered going to university. He said that passing Selection was very far from a certainty in spite of my Parachute Regiment background and I should have a strong and worthwhile Plan B. He also said that many soldiers left the SAS regretting having not educated themselves.

The catalyst that initiated the change was the act that got

me temporarily discharged from the reserves, but the build-up of disciplinary incidents had been long preceded by my feeling that I wasn't fully cut out or suitable for long-term service life. I was an individualist and a fanatical lover of freedom, but more than anything, I found it difficult to rein myself in when faced with the stifling routine and regulations of peacetime barrack life. Having a courageous tongue and little respect for authority were characteristics that didn't mesh well with army life and had got me into regular trouble. Gradually the way I saw myself, my colleagues and my future in the military system, in particular in the Parachute Regiment, began to change. It was ironic that the same inquisitiveness and sense of adventure that had led me to join the army in the first place would eventually push me in another direction. Regardless of my shifting perspectives and less than exemplary conduct, I had been an accomplished soldier and was still caught in a state of uncertainty as to whether I should return as a full-time soldier or not after university. I had enjoyed the physical challenge and learning specialist skills, but most of all I missed the camaraderie. I'd even gone as far as volunteering for the Royal Marine Commando Test to ingratiate myself with those who could facilitate a return to my former Naval Special Forces unit. The build-up training was to start in three weeks after the Christmas break, and as a reservist this time, I would still be able to maintain my studies. It promised to offer me the best of both worlds and I was excited.

As I left the city limits behind I was greeted with picture-book views of a timeless rural landscape, where medieval villages survived virtually untouched by the twenty-first century. There were no hedgerows and few fences, just field after field of browns and yellowy greens with the occasional dusting of snow, all interlocked in a rough patchwork of colours. Giant rounded hay mounds covered with roped-down tarpaulin dotted the fields in random patterns, and the villages and farmhouses also looked to be from a bygone age with windmills, watermills and here and there a horse-drawn cart. All my life I'd dreamt of visiting the Transylvanian wilds, a place Bram Stoker described as sinister and haunted, but instead I found myself looking at a world more reminiscent of Tolkien's Shire from *The Hobbit*. I took some photos from the train window, wishing I had something better than my crappy disposable camera.

An hour into the journey I caught my first glimpse of the mountains, a giant mass of rock and snow emerging from the tapestry of a multi-coloured landscape. The train veered off and I lost sight of them behind woodland and pockets of dead ground. When they came back into sight they looked magnificent and captivating; the edges of the peaks sharpened like daggers as the sun hit them from behind.

Rising above all but a few peaks of nearly equal height was Moldoveanu. At over 2,500 metres, it was the highest of the Fagaras mountains, which although proudly independent as a range, was part of the Carpathian chain stretching in a great arc for 1,500 kilometres from the Czech Republic to Romania and the Iron Gates on the river Danube.

At a rail junction further ahead, I noticed some tracks leading into a guarded military compound. The base roused my interest as I knew that a squadron from my old army unit had only recently trained in this very area. I had received a humorous report from a friend telling me their Romanian hosts were pretty sneaky, and during meal time one day they had sent a female cleaner to spy on the squadron's accommodation block. He joked that 'any soldier worth his salt knows nobody ever cleans up after you in the army, no matter how hospitable the host nation'. The cleaner went about her duties, and was eventually caught by the sentry as she attempted to examine and photograph the unit's secret UHF radio communication devices. 'Had she got away with it, the intelligence would have been in Moscow before we'd finished dessert,' he said.

Although it was all seen as a bit of a laugh, they knew not to turn their back on the Romanian army and its spies. This memory contributed to a sense of unease at odds with the exhilaration I'd been feeling.

I slept for a good part of the journey and when I woke the landscape outside had completely transformed. Rural charm had been replaced by a wild Carpathia of jagged mountains, deep ink-black forests and old stone forts with crooked battlements guarding secret corridors into the mountain valleys. I felt a mounting joy – this was the Romania I had come to see. This was a place of myth and legend, where the distant howl of the wolf still chilled the night air, where bears left their claw marks on the towering pines and the lynx lurked ghost-like among the high forests and crags. My excitement reached a crescendo as a scene that could have been straight from a *Dracula* film eerily presented itself. Strategically positioned on a rocky outcrop was a grim and mythical-looking old stone fortress with a solitary tower, surrounded by an evil-looking wood. All that was needed to cap the scene off was a flurry of bats, but it wasn't to be.

I'd always wanted to visit some of the castles connected with the Dracula myth, especially Castle Bran, supposedly the home of the titular character in Bram Stoker's *Dracula*. I'd read the book when I was thirteen years old but had been gripped by the myth since seeing Christopher Lee playing the count at an even younger age. I was eager to see the country for myself and connect the myth of Dracula to the legend of Vlad Tepes, or Vlad the Impaler, whose history had been incorporated with the fictional account of Dracula's past in

Stoker's original works. In a Bucharest museum I'd seen copies of old German woodcuts depicting Vlad's cruelty: feasting on steaks while his executioner cut off body parts of other impaled victims. Legend had it that the invading Ottoman army retreated in fright at the sight of thousands of rotting and impaled corpses lining the banks of the Danube.

Seeing Fagaras town in the distance I felt the early tingle of excitement and anticipation. After being cooped up in Manchester I couldn't wait to get stuck into the heart of the country and the bones of my trip. I would ski, climb, explore and hopefully encounter some wildlife. I had high expectations of Fagaras. The guidebook had said it was remote, traditional and beautiful, but then it had also said that Bucharest was the Paris of the East. To me Romania's capital had felt soulless, as if it had been eaten by Paris and vomited out as some vile grey northern town from back home thirty years ago. I'd been glad to leave. My first impressions of Fagaras weren't great either, the streets were smeared with old snow and everything in the immediate vicinity had an old, dirty and broken look about it. A huge factory on the edge of town scarred the landscape, with thick black smoke spilling from its towering chimneys, sending a cumulus of grey filth up into the sky and making the town seem darker than it really was.

A busy market ran along two of the side streets, finishing at the far end of the station. A bevy of red-faced women passed hurriedly by, balancing large bundles on their shoulders and carrying bright, colourful bags, heavily laden with wares. I walked over to one of the stalls and bought some chocolate, receiving plenty of friendly and curious smiles from everyone who passed me. A group of shifty-looking taxi drivers had followed me down into the market, and in recognition of my foreignness, took turns in offering me an array of rip-off prices to a 'very cheap' hotel they knew. I ignored their offers and walked back to the station car park where official-looking taxi drivers stood chatting, smoking and drinking coffee.

I approached the group and explained that I wanted to go into the mountains, repeating the name 'Moldoveanu' to make sure I was understood. A group discussion ensued over my destination with much tooth sucking and wild gesticulations to indicate that the roads would be snowed in, that only a fool would attempt such a journey and even then it would require a suitably mountainous fare. I looked at their shiny new cars and understood further efforts would be wasted – nobody with a nice set of wheels would be willing to risk it in the mountains. My best bet lay with one of the devious-looking characters who had followed me back up to assess my progress. I stood my ground and eventually managed to isolate one of them. They were like pack animals, far less fearsome when alone, especially when it came to negotiating. After much haggling and feigning of 'I'll go elsewhere', I managed to agree a price acceptable to both of us, which worked out at roughly eight English pounds in old Romanian lei. When it came down to the specifics of my destination, the driver's unofficial status became more evident. Beyond the village of Victoria he had no idea where he was heading. Despite showing him my map, which he studied intently, he obviously didn't have a clue.

My Bergen was squeezed into the boot and I jumped in the front of his car, an old green Dacia close to falling apart. As soon as we'd set off the driver started popping sunflower seeds on the car cigarette lighter, the empty shells of which had already filled the ashtray to the brim and were close to spilling over. The car reeked with the stale odour of cigarette ash and burnt shells, the radio was played on full blast, blaring out some bizarre and terrible song which he seemed to be enjoying. Despite the state of his death trap vehicle I couldn't help noticing how thoroughly cheerful he was, driving along, and munching away to the beat of the music after having secured what was probably a great fare. I was just grateful that he had been willing to take on the journey.

Leaving town we crossed over a part-frozen river and headed south towards the north face of the mountains. As we drove deeper into the countryside the tarmac ended and turned into dirt road with tall banks of snow on either side. The only metalled road through the Fagaras Mountains was the Transfagarasan, the famous highway that cut the range from north to south across the valley of Balea. Connecting Transylvania to Walachia, the route twisted its way up to 2,000 metres at its highest point, passing more than forty lakes. The highway lay a good hour's drive west from Fagaras during the winter months, and despite the network of aqueducts, bridges and tunnels bored through the mountain, the risk presented by avalanches, rock fall and the depth of snow on the upper reaches meant the road was closed from October to June. Not to be put off, after climbing Moldoveanu, I planned to hire some Nordic skis, fit on some skins and telemark my way to the top. Aside from the challenge, I wanted to go up to Castle Pionerai, which was constructed by Vlad Tepes and was considered the authentic Dracula's castle, unlike the more touristy Bran castle. Like today, the main obstacle would be getting there as the trekking routes in the Fagaras were always about 15 kilometres from the train station and no buses ran there. If all went well I could take a taxi as far up the highway as the snow line would allow and ski up from there. I was a mountain goat and loved going up, but coming down was sure to be a grand reward for my endeavours.

Our route into the Fagaras foothills lay along a far more minor route and the car was soon jolting and skidding as the conditions got progressively worse. I began to think we would never get through as I could tell that even a jeep would have had difficulty. The car soon began spinning and sliding across the road, almost completely out of control. My driver kept his foot down, somehow managing to stay on the road and avoid crashing or rolling the vehicle. His fingers still tapped on the steering wheel to the beat of music, while he continued popping his sunflower seeds and spitting the empty shells out of the window. He remained unflustered as the roads quickly turned from difficult to downright dangerous. I was sure they would soon become impassable, especially in this old car. It got to a point where I wouldn't have held it against him if he'd refused to go on, yet the old Dacia kept going. The driver made a series of half confident turns at each junction, beckoning me to indicate which way to go. I'd cut my map down to the area of the mountains and foothills to make it smaller, so I wasn't much use as a navigator. As for my driver, he was either taking lucky guesses or had a good instinct for direction.

The road eventually took us past a small military outpost. A soldier in a long grey trench coat stood guarding the front gate, carrying out his shift on sentry duty. The crazy driver skidded to a halt and asked me to wind down my window. I found the handle was missing, so opened the door instead. He leaned across me and shouted for directions over the blare of his radio and the still-running engine. The soldier yelled back, followed by some hand movements signalling the way. After a moment's pause, he began shaking his head while offering more advice. Even I could understand he was telling us the way was likely to be blocked. Fortunately my driver would hear nothing of it and we were moving again before I had even shut the door, keeping the revs up in a high gear so the wheels didn't spin. Shortly after, we hit a wide road covered in a thick layer of frozen slush. The conditions were so treacherous, I was convinced we would come off the road at any moment and end up in one of the deep trenches that lined either side. The car began sliding, lurching from one skid to another and at one point the driver lost all control, and we found ourselves travelling sideways towards the ditch at high speed. I locked my arms out and pushed against the dashboard, genuinely holding on for dear life. I could tell the driver was slightly concerned as it was the first time he'd stopped stuffing his face with sunflower seeds. I released an arm and grasped the plastic hand grip above my head, bracing myself for a crash that miraculously never happened.

Heading up into the foothills, the car began to struggle, making an orchestra of clanks and bangs while pouring a thick, black, oily smoke from its exhaust. After fifteen minutes the way levelled off and we passed through miles of dark forests with small clusters of mysterious wooden houses, hidden away in neat circular clearings. These were the final pockets of civilization where I had least expected them. A few kilometres after the last of these secret villages we came to a fork in the track. The driver beckoned me to make a choice while I checked the map, before he decided to take a right anyway. Beyond the turn off, the road began to twist and dip again, the terrain became wilder as the forest closed in around us, cloaking the narrow pass in its darkening shadows. After a short drive we passed two farmers talking at the side of the road. My driver skidded to a halt and reversed until the car was alongside them. They eyed us as though we were fools as we checked with them for directions, and then sent us back the way we'd come. As the driver skilfully turned his vehicle to face the opposite direction, I noticed a large wooden structure tucked into the far end of a clearing in the woods behind the two men. It was the last building I would see for four days.

Back at the junction, we took the other fork and continued for five minutes before the driver decided we had come far enough and pulled over to one side. Looking at me with sternness in his eyes, he spat out another sunflower shell and pointed towards the mountains. I didn't understand a single word of what he said, but he seemed to be warning me that the mountains were dangerous, especially these ones. After paying him the agreed fare plus a generous tip for his heroics on the road, he followed me out of the car and lifted my Bergen from the boot and onto my back, giving me a hearty slap on the shoulder as he did so. I liked the driver and admired his disregard for the road and its conditions. He could have backed out and dropped me short, but he finished the job and got me to the mountains. Just getting this far felt like a small victory. I shook his hand, then watched him going back down the road until the Dacia disappeared from sight, a dot of green in a wilderness of white. Minutes later I could still hear the engine being thrashed as he skidded and swerved his way home.

CHAPTER TWO

WILDERNESS OF WHITE

I remained where I had been dropped off for a couple of minutes and took in the landscape. Beyond me lay an infinity of immaculate snow, a winter wonderland of deep, dark forest dusted in white and the knife-edge peaks of the Fagaras. There was a sharp coldness in the air, and a particular quietness of the sort that can only be found in the mountains. There were no footprints except mine and the expanse of white icing was marked only by the occasional rabbit and squirrel prints which crossed the track in straight and purposeful lines. I scanned my immediate surroundings and listened intently, there was no sign of movement or evidence of human activity, the silence only interrupted by the whispering shuffle of loose powder snow being blown across the ground by sudden wisps of breeze. Elated, it felt as if I had the whole vast range to myself.

I removed my down jacket and put on a Gore-Tex

windproof over my thermal base layer. My plan was to attack the lower reaches to make good time so I would quickly warm up. After orientating my map and working out the rough location of my drop-off point, I took a compass bearing to my first objective, folded the map away and double checked all my zips and pockets before moving off. I started off slowly, building up to a pace that I could maintain for a lengthy period. I followed a snowed-over dirt vehicle track for the first few kilometres, stopping once to explore a narrow tunnel carved into the side of a cliff. Impressed by the neat stonework of the archway, I decided it must be of some importance, even though the dead bracken and other vegetation suggested it was long out of use. Still curious, I fixed on my head torch and dropped my Bergen at the entrance. I didn't go far before signs of weakness in its roof convinced me to confine my explorations to above ground.

I left the vehicle track not long afterwards and was soon on the forest trail, powering my way up steeply winding mountain paths. I drew great endurance and vitality from being among the mountains and trees. I liked to move fast, to touch rock and brush the hairgrass and pine branches that grew along the trail with my fingertips and bring the smell to my nose as if to feed off the scenery. Immersed in this natural world it felt great to be so light and agile; I wasn't weighed down by heavy loads, yet I felt I had enough to survive. There were unofficial rules about how you should climb and how much you should carry, especially when climbing alone, but I'd grown up in the mountains and felt highly accomplished, without ever losing respect for what they could give or take away. In the Alps I'd run up high peaks in seven or eight hours wearing trail shoes, shorts and a long-sleeved base layer, climbs that would have taken fully equipped and well-dressed climbers a couple of days to ascend and descend.

I was always aware that some people would see my actions as wild, reckless or irresponsible, but to really know yourself you have to be willing to put yourself in situations where you'd be vulnerable. I'd set myself a challenge. From experience I knew that the important thing was not to catch something, what really mattered now, and in life, is the pursuit and everything we can learn along the way. For the next couple of hours I became lost in the biorhythms of my breathing and the sound of my boots crunching through the snow, the metronomic placing of one foot in front of the other for a long period sending me into a trance. It was easy to forget the fact that I was making an effort, as I'd reached the level where intense physical exertion becomes an almost subconscious act. It is something truly soul cleansing and impossible to replicate under any other circumstance, as anyone who runs will understand.

After covering good height and distance, I broke through

the lower forest and was greeted by the main ridge of the Fagaras and the unmistakable trapezoid shape of Vistea Mare, Moldoveanu's lower summit. The main ridge of the Fagaras forms a massive spine, which extends west to east in a fairly straight line for more than 70 kilometres, never dropping below 2,000 metres over a distance of about 50 kilometres. Menacing and intimidating, the line of peaks came in and out of focus intermittently, becoming obscured behind the silent and silvery march of clouds and the snow dance of spindrift blowing in unpredictable storms across the upper slopes. Occasionally, the wind kicked up powder in such a frenzy that it began to twist as if being sucked into some invisible vacuum, forming a vortex of snow. At other times, strong gusts would lift the surface of a large area and carry it up and across the slopes, creating the effect of a micro snow storm even though there wasn't any falling from the sky. There was a potent push and pull in the very sight of the mountains which attracted and repelled me in equal measure.

As I marched on, absorbed in my thoughts and the challenge of the climb, a strange and inexplicable sense of danger and fear came over me, as if nature was giving me some advance warning of an imminent threat. There's an inevitable psychological baggage that comes with climbing alone and even the briefest consideration of all those iconic and tragic stories of injury and death and the obvious risks was enough to remind me of the perils involved. At the same time as this strange terror struck, a pair of little ravens flew over the forest's canopy screeching. They came to ground and landed a few feet away from me. One bird cocked its head to the side and crowed as it fixed me with a beady and sinister eye. Was this a bad omen? I carried on, more slowly and cautiously. My imagination had been roused, and I couldn't help thinking about extrasensory perception, which I had learnt about in the army. In the jungle, our instructors had made us aware that we should pay careful attention to strange feelings outside our normal range of senses. 'It might be a little feeling in your stomach or something activated in your mind, warning you that something is wrong. Don't ignore it, call a halt and let the patrol commander know.'

Now I had a feeling similar to the sense you sometimes get when someone is looking at you, and some inexplicable impulse causes you to turn directly towards them. Though I wasn't usually prone to fear, I began to wonder if this was a warning. I had come a long way and wanted to climb this mountain, I wasn't going to call it all off simply because of a presentiment. Nevertheless, I stopped several times to look back the way I had come, struggling to shake the feeling that some malevolent force hung over me.

The early part of the mountain route was a marked trail used for summer trekking, a relatively slow and gentle climb with many lazy switchbacks. In the summer it would have been teeming with walkers and climbers, but in winter, with freezing temperatures, frightful winds and deep snow on the ground, the Carpathian and Fagaras Mountains were deserted, left to the wolves, bears and lynx which made up nearly 50 per cent of Europe's big carnivores. Eager to shake off my earlier fears I broke into a run again, covering several kilometres in no time at all. Along the way, I passed several coloured markers indicating height and distance scales to three mountain refuges. Even though I had no plan to stay in them, their existence was reassuring. After an hour of solid work I reached a fairly flat and open section of high ground. The way ahead seemed to stretch on for miles with no feeling of it coming to an end. I ran as hard as I could and was in my element racing across the ridgeline, the scenery rushing by like a reel of spectacular film footage. I was ecstatic at the landscape's beauty, remoteness and the sudden freedom I felt. I kept running faster and faster without tiring, as though time and distance had no control over me – it was an incredible natural high.

I slowed to a walk as I reached a path marked by a blue painted indication arrow. The way was blocked with snow and probably hadn't seen a person since the autumn. Within a few hundred metres of the trail markers I passed a large mound in a small hollow. My attention was drawn to a double set of footprints leading away from rabbit holes burrowed into the mound. My first guess was that they belonged to a fox, but I realized they were noticeably bigger than any animal I was familiar with. I squatted down and put my fingers into the prints, just as I did as a child when tracking foxes across woodland and fields. The depth, size and spacing of the tracks told me they must have belonged to something bigger, most likely a wolf. The only other possible explanation was wild dogs, which are of equal size and more likely to move in pairs. I knew the chances of seeing a wolf were slim. As well as being shy and elusive, they covered ground faster than I ever could. Nonetheless determined and optimistic about the chances of seeing one, I set off following their prints, which were heading in the same broad direction as the route I wanted to follow. Encountering one in the wilderness was a dream of any nature lover, and wolves had a powerful influence over my imagination. I followed the prints for nearly half an hour, as they meandered wildly in and out of the trees and crisscrossed both sides of the ridge as if they too were chasing a trail.

By mid-morning I had gained an encouraging amount of height, but was yet to find a vantage point up onto the mountain. I was pretty much trailblazing my own route through miles of trackless forest, and despite my map and prior planning, some decisions could only be made on the ground.

I kept to the ridgeline and regularly scanned the sky and Moldoveanu's summit for changes in weather. The winds still blew forcefully on the upper reaches, although visibility remained good. As I found myself hoping the conditions would stay calm, it brought about an amusing reminder of my time in the army. During winter test marches on the Welsh mountains, there was a common DS (Directing Staff) joke in which, when a recruit approached their tented RV/checkpoint, they would pretend to establish radio contact with God. It went along the theme of standard military voice procedure:

DS: 'Hello, DS to God, over.'

After receipt of the imaginary response from God: 'Send over.'

DS: 'DS request rain, over.'

There were deviations in the climatic conditions requested, but typically they were for more rain and reductions in visibility. The joke was only amusing up to the point where it became apparent that God–DS relations were very strong indeed.

After putting the level ground behind me, I once again followed the marker arrows back into the darkness of dense forest. As I walked through a sharp and steep switchback that became rocky underfoot, I saw a wooden crucifix embedded in a square pile of rocks on the outside of the track's loop. An old, weathered blue raincoat and a plastic hard hat had been nailed to the cross. The sight of it brought about the return of my earlier instinctive fears and my sobering reflections intensified as I examined the inscription on the brass plaque, a memorial to climbers who had died on the mountain. I paused and touched it as a sign of respect and then moved on quickly, eager to leave my sense of foreboding behind.

It took another stretch of quick going to reach a position with good coverage of Moldoveanu's lower slopes. The only interruption to the ascent's uniform pattern was a man-made firebreak that left a white streak running through the blocks of dark trees. Although it looked very steep and tough to climb, the firebreak would provide a clear and direct route to the realms of the high mountains. To reach it I faced a tumultuous 300-metre scramble down and up a steep slope packed with dense vegetation and fallen trees. Growing up where I had done had helped me become a skilled negotiator of terrain, especially downhill, hurling myself over roots and logs and shifting scree. A lifetime of trail running, mountain climbing and six years military service and I'd never as much as sprained an ankle. With my Bergen straps pulled tight so that it sat high on my back, I took a rough surface bearing and began to bomb my way down and up again. After a damn hard slog, sometimes on my hands and knees, I broke through the cover of the trees and made an exhausted entrance onto the mountain proper.

CHAPTER THREE

CLIMBING FREE

I brushed the snow off the surface of a fallen tree and took a seat to recover my breath. I decided it would be a good time to eat the last meal of the day, as from then on I would rely on snacks to keep up my energy. Just as I was about to pour coffee from my flask, I closed it back up, deciding it was best saved for brief rest stops during the climb. I pulled out my cooking utensils and took control of the stove and prepared breakfast: warm porridge and hot drinking chocolate. Sitting snugly in my jacket, in the nest of a small natural hollow, I quickly sank into a state of comfort and relaxation. How often could a man dine so peacefully amid the forests and the mountains of Europe's last untamed wilderness? It was a unique, pure feeling to carry my bed and food on my back. A strong sense of freedom came from knowing I could go wherever I liked and sustain myself in the most basic way. Such simple pleasures had been extinguished by city life, so I now appreciated, savoured and understood what I was experiencing all the more. Enjoying my tranquil circumstances, I almost didn't want to get up and leave.

Following a good rest I packed my kit away tightly and made my first real steps up the mountain. I climbed in a straight line, digging my boot ends into the early morning snow, still hard and compact from the cold of the night. Being on the mountain worked different muscles to the inbound trek and for the early part of the climb it felt as though I was walking against a conveyor belt. I was breathing hard and had the sensation of going nowhere. Only by looking back down could I impress myself with the massive distances I was covering. I could see the uninterrupted trail of my footprints running all the way down to the trees from which I had emerged, leaving my mark on the mountain's surface. My route up channelled me through a firebreak about 15 to 20 metres wide, which offered me good protection from the side winds. The even nature of the slope favoured solid progress and for a good while I was able to gain a lot of height. The conditions were perfect, inviting me to launch my way up the slope. I took frequent brief rest breaks, just long enough to munch some snacks and take a swig of water. My progress made me feel relaxed and confident. The views of the mountains on the other side of the valley were spectacular, but seeing how high they were made me realize how much further I had to go.

It took a couple of hours hard going before I could make out the end of the firebreak. Distinguished against the backdrop of a clear white horizon and wedged between the staggering tree line, a shimmering cliff of ice and snow guarded a way up onto the mountain's upper reaches, an impressive gateway into the realm of the high mountains. I put in another stretch of solid climbing, curious to see what challenge this wall presented. As I neared the end of my channelled route, the gradient increased sharply, causing me to shift over to one side. I kept close to the tree line for safety and adjusted my climbing technique by dropping down onto all fours. Converging sections of the upper slopes funnelled down into a narrow channel like an egg timer, forming a natural avalanche chute. The convex nature of the slope above the ice wall, which looked to be about $30°$, increased the potential for avalanche as there was less compressive support for the snow pack and a greater tendency to wind load compared to concave or planar slopes. However, I was aware that avalanches could happen on any steep slope without thick anchors, whatever the incline's shape. The nature of the terrain under the snowpack was another variable for concern: smooth, grassy slopes are much worse at holding snow while rocks and trees can help anchor it. This meant that the firebreak was relatively safe, but a few hundred metres above the ice wall, the angle of the slope allowed snow to accumulate, yet was steep enough for snow to accelerate once set in motion by a combination of mechanical failure of the snowpack and gravity. The largest avalanches form turbulent suspension currents known as powder snow or mixed avalanches. They can exceed speeds of 300 km/h, and masses of 10,000,000 tonnes; their flows can travel long distances along flat valley bottoms and even uphill for short distances. I'd heard and read about the deaths of famous climbers but another more startling statistic from my Arctic warfare course stuck in mind. During World War I, an estimated 40,000 to 80,000 soldiers died as a result of avalanches during the mountain campaign in the Alps at the Austrian–Italian front, many of which had been triggered by artillery fire and bombing.

My assessment was confirmed when I caught sight of a small snow deposit as it spilt off the ice wall and hurtled down the slope, dispersing into powder and dying out long before reaching me. This was warning enough, if a larger spill or a big slab broke off I could be in trouble. I became increasingly cautious and refrained from my rapid, head down marching style. My eyes were now firmly fixed on all activity from above.

The potential for danger increased exponentially as I got closer to the ramp. The nearer I was to it, the less time I would have to react and withdraw into the trees. Although these snow spills were relatively small, their presence reminded me how vulnerable and isolated I was. A period of anxious concentration followed. It was always possible that I could move into the cover of the trees and attempt to make my way up through them, but the going would be slow and the idea seemed too much like cheating. Perhaps I was deliberately making things difficult for myself, but with the climb being far from technical, I was eager to make the most of the challenge that the firebreak provided, it was hard work and allowed me to feel I was really climbing. More than anything I wanted to experience the essential nature of being on the mountain, to enjoy its vast space, beauty and all its associated risks. If I ducked into the shelter of the trees, I'd deprive myself of the crunch of snow underfoot or that satisfying feeling of looking back across at the opposite peaks. I temporarily forgot about the summit and became totally absorbed in my task, embracing the present moment. This is what it was all about.

My progress had steadied to slow and cautious foot placements, but my consistent efforts soon paid off and I was at the base of the ice wall and about to put the firebreak behind me. The angle of the wall stood at 50°, with a bowl-shaped ledge halfway up. At about 15 metres in height, it was hardly a serious obstacle but coming down would be much trickier. Leaning into the slope, I kicked the front spikes of my crampons into the snow to test my hold and found good ice.

I climbed up the ramp quickly, crossing a small bowl section at the midway point and then attacked the rest of the wall by staying close to a rocky outcrop protruding from the tree line. As I neared the upper reaches I made a complacent move, failing to gauge correctly the report of my right crampon going into ice, which I should have recognized lacked the sound and feeling of a good foothold. A chunk of snow holding my foot fell away, causing the crampon to lose its hold with the weight I had committed. I fell sideways and then onto my back, sliding head-first down the ramp until I crashed to a stop. Luckily the bowl caught my fall, saving me from the full drop. Winded and in pain, it took a couple of minutes for the dizziness to fade, in which time I just lay on my back, content to rest. Lethargy quickly left me as I remembered the snow spill I'd witnessed earlier – I couldn't risk lying about in an area so obviously prone to avalanches. I pulled myself up sharply and wriggled on my stomach until I was a safe distance away from the ledge and climbed back up again.

A minute later I was in another world, my horizon stretched up in a massive expanse of huge white snowdrifts which had the look of giant meringues. It was more peaceful now that I had left the forest behind, the sound of the wind brushing against the trees was replaced by silence and calmness. I scanned the ground to my front looking for an easy route up to the ridge. The way ahead presented a series of convex slopes and snow drifts that rolled in like frozen waves. The immediate danger was snow spill, so I moved off into the side of the mountain following the upper edge of the forest. Once at a safe distance from the ramp I selected a rough line up and moved off, traversing in zigzag lines, dodging difficult sections in search of a friendlier route. It must have snowed recently as each step was taking a little bit more effort, with my boots sinking in the soft surface. I moved in small bursts with frequent stops to recover my breath. Pockets of deep snow and false summits quickly took their toll and after twenty minutes of fighting soft powder I turned my back on the summit and made a seat in the snow. The stop became prolonged enough for me to feel cold, prompting me to put on my warm kit and find somewhere comfortable to eat and rest.

Fifty metres to my front stood a dome-like structure where a lone fallen tree rested atop a huge boulder. Where it had caught a massive snowdrift from strong crosswinds, a cornice hung from the rock like a frozen wave curl, forming a small cave. On closer inspection, it looked an ideal place to rest and escape the wind, the only problem being that I needed to reach the shelf at the far end. A 2-metre deep cavity blocked my way, bridged only by the snow-covered fallen tree. I had to cross cautiously, searching out the solidity of the trunk underfoot to avoid being deceived by the snow-laden fir branches. In no time at all I'd fashioned out a snow chair and made myself comfortable in the best seat in the house. Looking out over the valley and at the peaks beyond, the scene was magnificent, a breathtaking panorama of snow spreading up beyond the greens and browns of the largest tract of unfragmented forest in Europe. I could still faintly see the black rocky peaks of the snow-covered mountains on the opposite side of the valley, fading in and out of focus through the distant snowfall. The range seemed to stretch on without end. In these moments I experienced a unique kind of elation and a true connection with the landscape. I was isolated, yet completely at ease.

I poured coffee from my flask and ate some dried fruit. The wind died and the air became filled with a sublime quietness. I sat motionless, hearing only my own breath and the beat of my heart. As I focused on my surroundings, a mild humming, the sound of silence rang gently in my ears. A rare and peaceful energy resonated across the slopes. The moment of stillness was followed by snowfall, soft heavy flakes that filled the sky and swirled down all around me. There was an enclosed sensation, like being inside a giant snow glass, the sort that comes alive when you shake it. Being so far away from everything allowed me to truly appreciate the wildness of the environment and recognize the extent of my separation from my day-to-day life. That was the great thing about Romania, I hadn't needed a park permit or permission to come here, nor was I required to be registered, assigned a date or a camping pitch. Liberated from rules, unchecked, unhindered and free, I could come and go as I pleased. The machinations of city life were far away and almost inconceivable, and for the time being, the shackles of society slipped away and any delusions of self-importance I might have had were blown away with the wind. This was as free as I would ever be. Sometimes one can experience happiness without recognizing it, here on my snow shelf, perched on the mountain ledge, I was not only genuinely happy, I knew I was.

Feeling strong after my coffee break I carefully left the snow cave. The snow was softer and much deeper, the air had cooled and the chill of the wind whipped against me as I gained height. The other side of the valley was now hidden behind the veil of thick snowfall and soon after the summit disappeared from sight too. Feeling enclosed by the weather, I stopped and quickly set a compass bearing. Over the next couple of hundred metres I laboured my way up, bogged down by ever deepening drifts of fresh powder. I withdrew from my course to the right, cutting diagonally across the slope, but my new line proved fruitless, with snow still reaching the top of my boots and in some places coming up to my knees. It seemed as if there was no way through. I decided to continue my advance in a straight line, judging that these conditions were due to the shape of this particular section of the mountain. I was optimistic of finding firmer ground higher up. Despite the difficult going the mountains put me under their spell and banished from my mind the hostel's party atmosphere and all the insignificant affairs and drowsiness of student life back in Manchester. This struggle in the snow with sinking boots and a weighty pack on my back, pitted against the formidable elements seemed a finer thing than keeping company with the other backpackers merry with festive cheer back at the hostel, indifferent to the mountains. The contrast roused no envy in my breast; I passionately loved my small but gallant place on this giant expanse of snow, rock and ice.

My intention had been to summit that day, with enough time to retreat back to the safety of the forest for the night. If necessary, I would finish the ascent in the early hours of the next morning, giving me enough time to make it back to Fagaras on foot. I knew it was important to stick roughly to schedule as I only carried limited supplies, but I decided I would break the unwritten rule and use up my emergency rations if I needed another day.

Upon reaching the next plateau the sky cleared briefly and revealed the ridge. Two or three more false crests now stood between me and a relatively easy route to the summit. Passing through a zone where there was good going underfoot, I hurried to make up for lost time. Slope conditions only remained favourable for so long before I was back in deep snow. Picking a route up was like walking through a minefield; intermittently I would take a hit, stepping into a deep spot and sinking up to my waist. I forced myself into making bounds of powerful exertion but the recovery I needed to make between each sequence of steps made it an ineffective tactic. A slower pace was just as energy sapping, the longer my feet remained in one place, the deeper I sank, and I was forced into a speed I was unable to sustain. The struggle reminded me of the extracurricular physical thrashings at Parachute Regiment training depot: running along the shooting range, laden with 35 pounds of webbing and rifle, jumping in and out of rain-flooded firing trenches, repetition after repetition until our legs turned to jelly.

A short distance ahead lay a fallen tree. I made my way towards it with the same desperation as a troubled swimmer trying to reach a life buoy. Stretching my arm out for the nearest branch, I pulled myself up onto the trunk. The first thoughts of a retreat came to me as it had been a tougher climb than I had imagined, a real gut buster. I could accept the difficulty of the task, but the going was just too slow. I faced up slope and mulled over my chances. The next crest was only 50 metres away and I wouldn't forgive myself if I didn't push on. I'd worked hard coming this far and would be damned if I was going to turn around.

'Summits are important,' I reminded myself.

A short while after moving off I was stopped in my tracks by an unusual sound, accompanied by what felt like a mild earth tremor shaking the ground directly beneath me. Perplexed and still rasping wildly for breath after my exertions, I thought perhaps I was hearing things or had confused whatever I thought I'd heard for the sound of my own movements. It started to snow again, much more heavily this time. I was moving so slowly that the sweat on my back had begun to freeze. Even though the wind had died down I couldn't get warm. As the weather closed in, I could no longer distinguish where the mountain ended and the sky began, all I could see was a uniform blanket of whiteness. I knew then that I had to go down, so I pulled out my compass and added 3,200 mils, converting to a back bearing so that I could take the same line down that I had taken up, an essential measure as I couldn't see more than 10 metres down the mountain. There was no way I could summit, my sole objective now was to get down safely. After only a few steps I heard the noise again, this time recognizing it to be the slide of recent snowfall putting stress on the existing snow pack. The sound travelled across the upper reaches of the mountain and then cut out abruptly. I remained still, straining to listen in nervous anticipation. Shortly after it happened a third time, flooding the slopes with an eerie sound as if the mountain itself had creaked. I felt alarmingly close to the epicentre of these jolts. If this was building up to an avalanche, there wasn't a chance in hell I could avoid it. I was massively exposed on an open slope, escape was impossible.

Ignoring the fact that it was bad mountain practice, I removed my crampons, dropped down onto my backside and started to toboggan. It was hardly a legitimate manoeuvre but I was fright-stricken and knew I had to get down fast. I bombed my way down, pushing off with my arms and drawing my legs in and out to keep up momentum when the gradient decreased or I hit pockets of deep snow. As I slid, I kept glancing over my shoulder to see if anything was happening behind me. As I distanced myself from the sound, I felt relieved and then, a moment later, disappointed because I had turned back. I wondered if I could have pushed on a little more after having been so close to the ridge.

It was just as I was making my way to a safe spot to bivouac further down the mountain that the terrifying crack of an avalanche being triggered forced me to look back up the slope from where I had come. I should have run immediately but my mind was stuck in shock mode. Some part of my brain wasn't processing effectively, as though the transmitters that should have been activated by danger were failing to send the appropriate commands to the rest of my body. The charge, energy and noise of Mother Nature in full force had me transfixed, I guess it was perverse; I just wanted to keep on looking at it. Compelled to stare, it was almost as though I had to see it to believe it. When my mind escaped its shocked trance, I turned towards the side of the mountain and ran for my life. The avalanche was heading straight for the firebreak. My only chance was to get as deep as possible into the cover of the trees and hope they would break up the force and divert the flow of snow. As soon as I was wide of the ice wall, I cut straight down into the forest and began weaving my way through the trees, desperately seeking out a clear path to make good my escape. Each second passed like a minute, my stomach churned with fear and I could feel the veins in my neck pulse as they struggled with the sudden overload of blood traffic. The noise built up behind me and I could feel the earth tremor beneath my feet. Hurdling deadfall and rocks strewn across the forest floor disrupted my balance and control, sending my head faster than the rest of my body. I recoiled and rebounded from tree to tree, banging my knees and elbows in a sequence of bruising encounters. Branches clawed me back by snagging on my jacket and Bergen, it was only momentum that kept me going. How I didn't fall I don't know.

I didn't need to look back, I felt sure it was going to hit me, the noise was like a wing of bombers coming over followed by the machine-gun rattle of snapping branches and the spray of powder snow that quickly filled the air all around me. The intensity of the moment was immense, it felt as though my insides were trying to jump out of my body. I thought I was going to vomit.

Then . . . nothing. The avalanche passed and continued its destructive charge down through the firebreak. I kept running, securing myself deeper into the safety of the trees, as far away as possible from where it had all happened. When I was sure I'd escaped I came to a stop and suddenly felt embarrassed as though I'd got lost in my own house. I steadied my nerves and tried to take in what had just happened. Muscles twitched randomly in my body as I began to laugh, a nervous reaction interrupted by simultaneous hiccup-like gasps to regain my breath. This was the first time terror had truly gripped me since childhood.

I removed my sun glasses and the orange tint to my surroundings was gone, it was beginning to get dark. The transition had been overwhelming: one moment serene beauty and tranquillity, followed by the sudden shift to cataclysm. To experience that fine line between life and death was the ultimate reality check. All day I hadn't been able to escape the feeling that something bad would happen, and even though everything had been going smoothly, there was always that instinct telling me to look out. I started to think that it had perhaps been a mistake not to have begun my descent earlier. I should have taken notice of my intuition, my body had been talking to me, sending butterflies into my stomach and tapping at some part of my brain telling me to turn back. Cold, tired, stubborn and driven, I'd been filled with a fearful desire to reach the summit and had unremittingly pushed on. I'd been guided by a different mindset up there, as if something in the air had changed everything. Down below, looking up at the peaks, it all seemed so bloody stupid and pointless.

As darkness loomed, I precariously made my way down the mountainside, firmly holding onto thoughts of my sleeping bag, hot tea and a boil-in-the-bag meal. Although the initial shock of the avalanche had left me, the sense of impending disaster remained. A sense of urgency told me I needed to lose as much height as quickly as possible and find a suitable basha site, somewhere reasonably flat, free from rock fall and safely away from the course of another avalanche. Avoiding the exposure of the firebreak would cost me valuable daylight time, the forest floor was littered with loose rock and fallen branches, lending further danger to sharp and unexpected drops. The day's effort began to take its toll as I cut further into the forest. I was already shattered from going up the mountain, the last hours of the climb had been time consuming and energy sapping. Now I couldn't move fast enough to keep warm as the conditions underfoot were becoming treacherous. Amidst the trees were hidden ledges and sudden drops, and from behind me falling rock and snow crashed down off the top of small cliff faces. The noise informed me of the forest's imminent dangers and was a reminder of why most accidents happened going down. Picking a route required attention and patience. With no obvious or direct line of descent, the safest route drew me diagonally down into the side of the mountain. Although I came across a number of potential LUP (laying-up position) sites, I wasn't satisfied they were right, so I kept going down. It had been twenty minutes since the avalanche, another twenty and I would lose any remaining light the day had to give. The evening chill caused me to shiver and my tired and ill-coordinated efforts quickly started to tell. I was falling every 30 metres or so and my feet were regularly taken away by shifting scree that displaced into small rock slides as I walked across the slope. Branches painfully caught my face and eyes and annoyingly snagged my Bergen and jacket so that I had to go back to free myself. I'd soon had enough and decided at the next half decent place I would stop for the night.

The trees spread out in front of me, gradually opening into a clearing. As I crossed this open zone I looked back up the mountain: small snow spills cascaded off a wall of rock and ice a couple of hundred metres away from where I stood. Beyond this feature I had a clear line of sight up to the darkening edges of the summit. In an instant, I stopped being so disheartened, my mood lifted and my optimism returned at the prospect of a second attempt the next day. As I turned back down the slope, I was stopped in my tracks by the same distinct crack and echo as I'd heard before, followed by the thunder of moving snow surging down the mountain. My body froze, a wall of sound, energy and snow from high up the slopes was heading straight for me, catching me completely exposed. It wasn't anywhere as near as big or deep as the first avalanche but still powerful enough to wipe me off the slope. Escaping my petrified state, I turned and sprinted, racing straight for the trees. Knowing it would get me escalated my fear to mind-numbing levels, it was only a matter of how soon and how hard the avalanche was going to hit me.

The next thirty seconds were of pure violence, my heart rate had gone into the red and my body was tumbling forwards, totally out of control. As the avalanche came up behind me I was sprayed in a whiteout mist of snow particles. Blinded and off balance, my pack came up over my head and pushed my neck down. Floundering in deep snow, I fell heavily and rolled into a sequence of head-over-heels. The instant I got back to my feet I was engulfed in a shower of snow and ice and smashed off balance. In frantic leg and arm movements, I began kicking and paddling in a swimming motion, trying to keep afloat to stop myself going under. Thoughts of being buried alive flooded my head, quickly followed by a recall of my avalanche drills from the Marines. I had to dribble, if I was buried and became disorientated, I wouldn't know which way was up, down or sideways. Gravity would take the saliva down. If it ran up my top lip and nose, I should dig the opposite way.

The force flicked me up and down like a ping-pong ball as I kept up my vigorous arm and leg movements. It was like being caught in bad surf – there is not much you can do except try to survive. I braced myself for an impact, I believed I would be smashed to pieces or crushed before being buried alive but, seconds later, the pressure beneath me had gone and I became aware of a different and even more petrifying sensation. I was falling – the avalanche had blasted me off the ledge of a cliff.

I was seized by a rush of terror so powerful I felt as if my head was cracking. My stomach lurched and moved up inside my body in protest at the force of gravity. Cascades of snow followed me down, huge lumps flew past my head, I was aware of some of it hitting me. I was in flight long enough to have thoughts, but after a few seconds I stopped understanding anything. Real time stood still and I just waited, convinced that I was about to meet my end.

The fall lasted perhaps five seconds before I landed with a colossal whack. All the air was knocked from my lungs and the crack of my breaking bones rang out like a ridiculous action-movie-punch sound effect. I hadn't stopped, the momentum of my fall took me further down the slope as all command over my body was lost. Loose-limbed and floppy as a rag doll I slid across the forest floor, clattering into trees, rocks and deadfall. Soil poured down my neck and inside my clothes as items in my rucksack tumbled along beside me. When I came to a standstill, I lay motionless, open-mouthed and unable to breathe. Stars flew round my head and strange bursts of electric blue light streamed into my eyes. I didn't know if they were open or closed or if my tongue and teeth were still in my mouth. I was floating out of myself and couldn't think in actions or words. Spinning, my consciousness began to fade.

CHAPTER FOUR

FIRST NIGHT IN THE OPEN

I don't know what came to me first, the violent convulsion of a breath or the spasm of shooting agony. Fortunately, a shock trance mercifully follows trauma, shutting the brain down to its most basic functions and removing you far enough from yourself to withstand the pain. I stared out blankly into the darkness, unmoving, uncaring and unprompted by any mental or physical desire to escape from the state I was in. Snowflakes fluttered through the canopy of the treetops, some landing gently on my face and hands. I could feel their cold, soft touch as they settled upon me even though I couldn't see them. I rose nervously up into a sitting position and began looking around, trying to assess my situation. Something wasn't right. I waited a few moments until I had regained my breath and tried to stand. My left leg gave way instantly, sending out an excruciating jet of pain, the worst I had ever felt. I attempted to ignore the realization of what had just happened and tried to stand again. As I put some weight through the leg I heard the scrape of bone against bone and felt another flash of horrendous pain. The leg gave way and I fell forward, sliding head-first down the slope while soil rushed down the front of my jacket and into my mouth. My injured leg snagged on something and another jolt of burning pain shot through me. I screamed and reacted instinctively by grabbing my leg instead of protecting my head or trying to brake with my hands. My body slammed hard against a tree, leaving me totally shell-shocked. I lay sprawled on the ground, head pointing down slope, capable of no more than breathing.

When I recovered my senses I attempted to move, shifting in small increments until my feet pointed down slope. It was an agonizing procedure that I was unable to carry out with the delicacy it needed. I nearly started sobbing, but shame made me pull myself together. Shuffling backwards, I secured myself on the up slope side of a tree to avoid sliding down again. Running my hands up and down my injured leg, I began exploring from ankle to groin. There were no unusual protrusions or noticeable deformations.

Was it broken? I tried not to answer the thought.

I could feel my feet and wiggle my toes, which was a good sign. By way of comparison I examined my good leg with my hands, noticing various bumps and lumps that had probably been there all my life. I switched back to my damaged leg and pressed searchingly into the bones and muscles. The leg throbbed so horribly that I couldn't determine exactly where the pain was coming from, it hurt in different places at different times. I feared multiple breaks or fractures. Finding no obvious signs of trauma, I decided to test out my range of movement to locate the break site. I moved the leg from side to side in careful inch by inch movements and attempted to bend the knee with fingers interlocked behind my leg. The action was answered with more searing pain and I knew then it was broken. Initially the implications of this situation failed to invoke any extreme emotion or reaction in me. I accepted it quite matter of factly, and still in a state of high shock I sat doing nothing useful. Fumbling around in the dark, I noticed my hand was wet and sticky. I put a finger to my mouth and tasted blood. I removed my knife and just as I made a rough guess at the wound site and was about to make the cut, I stopped myself. Why ruin the trousers? I closed the blade back into its handle, rolled carefully onto my good side and pulled my trousers down. There was a 2- to 3-inch wound on the top side of my left leg; the size of the opening made me uneasy. I carried an army issue first field dressing, which could absorb a pint of blood. I wrapped the dressing tightly and tied off the ends. Covering the wound made me feel better, the feel of so much of my own blood had made me queasy. I rolled onto my side again, pulled my trousers back up and wiped my bloody hands on my jacket. Job done, I resolved to think no more of it. I sat relieved, ruminating and gathering my senses, when it occurred to me that I'd come out of the whole thing relatively unscathed. Unnecessarily proud of myself, I spluttered out a giggle and then felt embarrassed. I had to convert my confused state into a plan and switch to a more disciplined mode of thinking.

I propped my back up straight and calmly ran the sequence of disastrous events through my mind. I had lost all my equipment and supplies as at some point during the fall or avalanche I had become separated from my rucksack and all its contents. I searched through my jacket and trouser pockets to see what I had, just to reassure myself that nothing had fallen out. In my jacket pockets I had a Leatherman tool, Silva compass, a length of para cord, a large bag of mini sausage rolls and another of sugar-coated cakes, both now reduced to crumbs. My jacket stank of lighter fuel from where the plastic casing of my cheap Bic had cracked, leaking away its contents into the fabric. I also had my favourite pair of football shorts – Brazil World Cup 98 – which I had carried for luck. I examined the emblem and ran my fingers over the four gold stars, thinking how useless they were in this situation, as well as being an awful good-luck charm. Since I'd lost my hat, I put them on my head and drew the waist cord around my crown. In my trouser pocket I still had my map, disposable camera, chocolate bars and mobile phone. I had been reluctant to bring the latter and only did so I could play Tetris in my sleeping bag at night. I turned it on knowing there would be no signal. There wasn't.

I then ran a mental check of all the important kit I no longer had: sleeping bag, bivi bag, poncho, army rations, dry kit, water bottle, flask and stove. All the essentials I needed to survive and a few extras like matches and the first aid kit were gone. The loss of my sleeping bag would hurt the most. I wondered if I would be able to get through the night being so exposed, as everything I was wearing was wet except for my jacket. I had little more than the clothes on my back and the shorts over my head. I shuffled round, turning my attention back up the slope to where I thought I had fallen. I couldn't distinguish between ground and space, there was nothing but blackness beyond the outlines of the nearest trees. I kept scanning, trying to determine how far I had fallen. It had felt like a big drop. Then something caught my attention, a small light from up slope bounced off a rock, emitting a faint ghost-like glow. I closed my eyes and looked away before returning my gaze. It was my head torch.

The discovery was immensely reassuring. If I could re-trieve it, the chances were I would find other kit scattered nearby. I just hoped my Bergen had been thrown over the cliff with me. The distance didn't look too far to deter me, but my body would surely protest. With a painful yelp, I rolled over onto my front and pulled my good leg forward. Lifting my chest off the ground, I transferred all my weight onto the knee of my mobile leg and moved my hands forward. My injured leg hung uselessly and pulsated in agony, forcing me to a stop after only a single push. After recovering, I clenched my jaw and repeated the movement, keeping a lower profile to the ground to relieve my leg of its dead and hanging weight. I coaxed myself forward with firm instructions: good leg forward . . . lift . . . and push . . . I covered 5 metres before collapsing into a heap again. I lay with my eyes closed attempting to escape what I was going through. Looking back up the slope, I saw the light again. I had quickly forgotten my objective.

'Get a grip, keep moving!' I sternly ordered myself.

Sinking my fingers into the earth, I clawed my way forward in an uninterrupted full-frontal assault on the slope. The soil beneath me was cold, hard and lumpy and thin skins of ice cracked as I wormed my way across the ground. After 15 minutes and not seeming to get any closer, I was beginning to get frustrated, even though I knew perceived distances could be deceptive in the dark. I kept my eyes fixed on the light and gradually inched my way towards it, moving diagonally to maintain traction. After a number of big hauls, I reached what I guessed to be the midway point. My dragging motion automatically became bolder and quicker, heightened by the possibility of being reunited with my equipment. In a moment's lapse of concentration I lost my foothold and started to slide down the slope. Reacting by instinct, I dug the boot of my injured leg into the ground. A bolt of blazing heat and pain caused me to cry out and my capacity to stay on the slope was finished. I paddled manically with my arms and kicked frantically into the earth, but to no avail. I was sliding uncontrollably and attempts to hold on only disturbed my descent, sending me tumbling into a backwards head-over-heels and eventually coming to a stop near to where I had started. All my efforts had been undone in an instant. I lay still, more sad than afraid as the chilling coldness of the ground seeped up through my clothes and into my bones. A night without my sleeping bag would probably finish me off.

'That's it then,' I thought, 'I'm fucked!' It hurt to think that I had failed.

Twenty minutes later I reached the point where I had slipped again. I admired this quality in myself: too stubborn or stupid to know when I was beaten. This time there could be no mistake, if I didn't get up, I never would. I kicked my boot hard into the ground three or four times until I was absolutely sure I had a firm hold. I pushed off, reaching out to grab a nearby tree. With a firm grip around the trunk, I pulled myself up with assistance from my right leg. I had to fight against the impulse to move the injured one, which went against any sort of natural movement as I wanted to put some weight through it to push myself up. I repeated the process several times, moving from tree to tree until I was within a couple of body lengths' distance from my torch. As I closed in, the boot of my injured leg got caught on a tree root. I tried to jerk it free, but couldn't get the damn boot over. The snagging motion was excruciating. I would have to let go of the tree to liberate myself. The instant I released my grasp, all the pressure went through my legs as I slid down. I heard the crunch of broken bones and felt an intensity of pain as they were now being pushed back into the joint instead of pulled. I thought I was going to faint. Amidst the chaos of my descent, I was able to catch a hold of a tree trunk, preventing myself from falling any further. The subsiding agony caused me to groan in pleasure as the stress was relieved from my leg.

I took a few minutes' rest and tried again. Taking up a handful of trouser material, I performed a sharp flip over onto my right side, sitting the bad leg on top of the good one. I started pulling up, hanging sideways from the tree, scraping along the ground until I was within reach of the tree root. It required a sharp, upward jerk from the bottom leg to jump my ankles over the obstacle. Another 5 metres and I was pulling myself clear and safely away from the possibility of slipping back down. As the immediate vicinity became relatively flat, I lifted my chest from the ground and made a series of consecutive heaves in the direction of the torch. I put my hand on something soft, wet and familiar, it was the woollen hat my mother had knitted for me. I removed the Brazil shorts from my head and replaced them with the hat. Within a few minutes, I also had my torch. It was a small victory, but it felt like something bigger. In all, it had taken me nearly two hours.

Leaning heavily into the rock and fighting to recover my breath I was glad to rest my overused arms. I turned off the torch to save power but the disappearance of light somehow made me insecure, as though I had lost my only means of protection. I flicked the switch back on and shone the beam onto my hand, studying its back and front intently as if it were some fascinating alien object. I wasn't sure if this was just an act of my delirious state, or perhaps I was confirming the reality of what was happening to me. I had to see the flesh of my hand and moving fingers to convince myself it wasn't all a bad dream. It took me some moments to snap out of my stupor of unsoldierly thoughts and do something useful. I dropped my trousers down to my ankles and placed the torch in my mouth, angling the beam onto my leg. It was encrusted with dried blood, otherwise it looked and felt normal to the touch. I still couldn't determine exactly where the break was, but figured it was most likely at the top since I'd landed on my backside. The pain throbbed from deep within and was not how I imagined a break to feel, but then I had never broken anything before. I thought it might be my hip, rather than my leg, or perhaps both. I decided against re-examining the wound, not wanting to disturb the well-placed dressing. I only had the one, and didn't want to waste it.

With no obvious plan about what to do next, and no immediate tasks to occupy myself with, I began to dwell on my situation. Things were no better than before and getting up here had only left me exhausted. A blur of time passed lost in a fog of uncertainty, then my mind drifted off, leaving my imagination open to all manner of scenarios in which I would meet my end. I suddenly felt trapped and very alone. The bitter cold gave me a kick. The longer I remained inactive, the more the frigid night air cut into me. I had to concentrate and not let my mind wander. Even though my body was broken, I still had my wits about me and reminded myself that when a soldier faced a problem he had to think and act. I dragged myself round the rock and pointed the torch beam up the slope expecting to see the cliff, but the light disappointingly disappeared into the darkness. I shone the torch around the immediate area, certain I must be close to where I fell and hopeful that some valuable item from my pack had been scattered nearby. Unsure how far I had rolled down, I contemplated going further up. Before making a move, I played out various courses of action and their likely outcomes. I figured I could last about three days before freezing to death, maybe not even that long without medical treatment. My best chance of survival was to find the sleeping bag – I could always get by without food and the rest of my equipment – cold was my fiercest enemy. I would probably have to wait for daylight to extend my search for it though.

The idea of going further up the slope was demoralizing. For all I knew, my Bergen could still be at the top of the cliff, hanging from a tree or buried under snow. I had no choice, it was fifteen below zero and I was already a shivering wreck. If I didn't find my sleeping bag, the cold would take me. But even if I miraculously made it up the slope and found my Bergen, then what? Sit in it and wait in the pathetic hope of rescue. Suddenly, both my Bergen and sleeping bag took on limited appeal. I knew that I could probably last a week if I could locate my supplies, but the horrors of that eventuality didn't bear thinking about. I wasn't going to be seduced into death by a sleeping bag and a disgusting army-issue ration pack. I decided that if I found the sleeping bag, I would keep moving while I was still capable. I could easily drag it down the slope with me. There was a stream at the bottom of the valley and a track within a couple of clicks. I believed I could cover the distance, and from there I could drink and shout for help. All I had to do was get through the night.

As I had not moved for half an hour the cold was now attacking me severely. The more I thought about it, the chances of finding my supplies seemed increasingly improbable. It would be much easier to make my way down the mountain as nobody would find me up here, but toughing out the night without the sleeping bag didn't appeal either. Whatever I decided, nothing altered my general situation. The choice between staying or keeping moving equated to one between stagnation or suicide. Making a decision became complicated, each choice a nightmare of conundrums with dire consequences. Trapped by indecision, I totally lacked the inclination to take any action. Maybe it was the cold and injuries hindering my ability to think and react. My memory began pulling out well-worn army maxims and training techniques, as if my brain deferred to them as my best bet for staying alive.

'Don't stand still, move and innovate, or die.'

I turned the torch back on and made my first few moves up the slope. I hadn't gone far before the ground became strewn with smooth, flat stones covered in moss and ice – rock fall from the cliff face. Making my way through was difficult, stones against knees and elbows hurt, even resting was uncomfortable. Nature's litter had turned into an enemy. My perception of my surroundings had shifted so dramatically, hours before all this had seemed so perfect and in its place, and I'd almost felt as if I were part of the landscape. Now the connection had been lost, everything was hostile, hurting me, slowing me down or becoming an obstruction. I busied myself trying to formulate a plan, but all ideas were contingent on finding my sleeping bag. I promised myself that if I found it, I would resist the temptation of making a full search for my other provisions. I would briefly investigate the immediate area at first light then make my way down as quickly as possible.

I switched the torch light from the ground to the space in front of me, the beam shone against the surface of a rock wall less than 10 metres away. I pulled myself energetically forward and directed the beam upwards, expecting to see how far I had fallen. Something wasn't right, I was at the foot of a small wall with a ledge about 2.5 metres in height. I knew my fall had been much greater. I hadn't reached the cliff at all, just a wall that appeared insurmountable. Keeping one hand planted on the ground and the other pressed against the wall, I nervously began to lift myself. I could feel bones adjusting position, initiating pain in hot flares as I pushed up to a standing position. My good leg began to buckle under my weight, tipping my precarious balance forward. I cried out as my forehead smashed into the hard surface, causing blood to pour down the bridge of my nose, and then spread across one side of my face. I wiped myself clean with the sleeve of my jacket and leaned back into the wall. With up-stretched arms, I attempted to hook my fingers over the ledge but it was just beyond my reach. I tried again, hoping the first stretch had put some length into my spine. I had no chance and even if I had, it would have taken a superhuman effort to pull myself up.

I shone the torch along the wall to both sides, hoping for a deviation in the ledge or an entrance up onto it by way of a gap or ramp. The structure was uniform on either side for as far as the light of my torch would stretch. I felt too exhausted to explore but another of the overly used army instructor proverbs jumped into my mind. 'Time spent on reconnaissance is seldom wasted.' Bastards!

I dropped back down to the ground and followed the wall to my right. Within 30 metres a barrier of large rock formations blocked my way, so I boxed round it and pressed on, scanning the ground for lost kit as I went. My torch saved me from another fall where the ground dropped away sharply, forcing me closer against the wall. I directed the torch above me. Rock stretched up beyond the reach of the beam and there was still no way up. I thought that maybe this was the cliff, but realized I could have dragged myself back up the mountain at totally the wrong angle. With only the one working leg my appreciation of time and distance was wildly inaccurate, I simply had to move in straight lines and go wherever my sense of direction took me. Running events through my mind I knew that finding the hat had been a good marker and that I was roughly on the course of my fall. With this in mind, I returned to my starting point with renewed intentions of getting up onto the ledge.

Back up on my good leg, I probed the rock face for holds big enough to take a boot end. There was nothing that would give me any leverage as my boots were big and bulky, hardly suitable for picking my way up a wall. There were a few finger holds at least. Now that I was standing, I noticed the peculiar sensation coming from my injured leg once the pain had subsided. It hung like a dead and heavy weight, over which I had limited control. I forced it to swing a little, pain informing me when I exceeded the willingness of its range of movement. I softly lowered the sole of my boot onto the ground, ensuring it bore no weight. For a second it was almost as if everything was OK and I could just walk off any time I chose. But some broken part of me that I couldn't see was stopping me from calmly making my way back down the mountain. In spite of my condition I decided I would try to walk anyway. I just hoped I could absorb some of the pressure away from the break site with my knee bent, at least long enough for a quick, small step. Wincing before I had done anything, I took a deep breath and tried to force a step. A tremendous streak of agony shot through my leg and I would have collapsed if I hadn't been leaning into the wall. So that was that. I was walking nowhere. I swore loudly like I always did when I felt pain or frustration. I was having difficulty accepting the trauma to my leg, the disability disgusted and angered me.

Edging closer to the wall, I felt around for finger holds above my head. There was nothing on the lower section, so I had no chance of securing a toe hold. Pressing my chest into the wall, I reached up and my left hand successfully searched out a crack. It was only enough to take three fingers, from tips to the first crease, but the right hand searched out a more profound hold. I readied myself, raised my good heel until on tiptoes and pushed off until I was hanging. I kicked and scraped my boot into rock face, urgently trying to find a placement while my injured leg hung uselessly and pulled me away from the wall. In the nick of time I found a sliver of a hold, it took nothing more than the rubber grip at the front end of the boot. I had to make a quick move as my arms were shaking with fatigue and I could feel myself coming off. I steadied myself and tried to breathe. I kicked off to execute the move, but there wasn't enough space to create the necessary upward momentum. I came away from the wall, falling into a horrible backward landing. Screaming agony into the night, I writhed on the ground in manic movements trying to free my broken leg which had folded beneath me and become trapped under my ass. The pain boiled so intensely it was unbearable, leaving me unable to direct or coordinate any movement to the limb. I was sure I would faint. Eventually I rolled onto one side and managed to pull it out straight with my hands. I was nearly sick. As the pain lessened, I stared up into the depths of the night sky, not even waiting for something to happen, just content to allow time to pass. It had been a pathetic effort but it was all I could manage. At least my failure made things easier and in part came as a relief. With choice now taken away from me, I would have to make my way down the slope and find some place safe to rest and wait for daylight. Leaving without the sleeping bag was my main concern, even in good weather a night in the open requires stamina. I was now committed to my unknown end.

The next move was to find a safe route down. I felt strangely unnerved being so close to where I had fallen and wanted to leave the place as quickly as possible. I carefully decided on the best method of descent, then with the torch beam angled to hit the ground just in front of my boots, I lifted the bad leg and placed it on top of the other, crossing them over at the ankles. I set off cautiously, feet first in an upright position and was quickly able to improvise an effective method of sliding down. Planting the heel of my good leg firmly into the ground, I could shuffle along by gradually bending the knee until my backside hit the heel of my boot. The manoeuvre could be carried out with minimum disturbance to the injured leg but any lapse in concentration was met with a torrent of pain. I focused on picking the easiest way down, although it was frequently worth the struggle to go directly over obstacles as going round them used up too much energy.

After an hour I realized I was only moving because I didn't know what else to do and the idea of stopping scared me. Weariness had started to overcome me and the will to keep going was dying. The forest floor was becoming increasingly difficult to negotiate and the danger exponential. Extreme exhaustion was overtaking my pain and the early signs of hypothermia were already upon me. Worst of all were my feet, they had become unbearably cold and the ends of my toes no longer had any feeling. I pushed on looking for a safe place to stop, knowing it would be suicide to continue much longer. The torch revealed a large fallen tree lying across the slope, it was as secure a place as I could hope to find. Clearing an area free of stones and twigs, my hand brushed over something that made a ruffling sound. Under torchlight I discovered it was my canoe sack. Inside was a spare pair of navy issue Norway socks with the distinct red band at the top, some underpants and a litre plastic water bottle just under half full, the weight of which had brought down the canoe sack. It was a worrying thought that my Bergen had been so easily ripped open and its contents chucked so far down the mountain, but it heralded hope that more of my kit was scattered nearby.

As soon as I had secured my position against the tree

trunk, I began to administrate myself. My immediate priority was my feet, which were in a bad way; the sensation in my right foot had almost passed beyond pain and gone into a dullness I mistrusted. My foot felt grossly swollen, as though it was going to explode. A convulsing throb had begun working its way up my leg and had now reached my calf, so that pain was attacking the injured leg in both directions. If the break had cut off the circulation of blood to my foot, the tissue would die and there would be a real risk of gangrene setting in, so I knew I had to remove the boots as quickly as possible. A desperate struggle to unpick the frozen bootlaces followed as I couldn't feel the knot. My numb fingers were useless, able to do nothing more than tug when I felt the sensation of lace between them. Although the knot eventually slipped, the tightness remained. I pulled and twisted my foot with as much force as I could muster and still it wouldn't budge. I set about removing the lace with the pliers on my Leatherman tool, but it wasn't enough to free my foot. Something more aggressive was required, so I jammed the boot heel behind a tree root, trapping it so that I could pull my leg towards my body. It needed plenty of force before it would move even slightly. At first it was millimetres, a second yank and the heel slipped. A third and the boot came off along with my sock which had frozen to the interior of the boot's fabric lining. I peeled it out and placed it in my trouser map pocket so heat from my thigh would dry it out. My foot was marble white and cold to the touch. I tried to revive some feeling by giving it a gentle massage, and once the cold air had dried the clammy skin, I put on a fresh sock and continued to knead the foot with my thumbs. It took some time before the first tingling sensations arrived, the steady return of circulation felt strangely pleasurable.

The pliers had the other lace out within a couple of minutes. I figured the secret was to wedge the heel and divert the pressure through a bent knee. The slightest tension initiated pangs of white-hot pain, causing me to break out into weak sobs. I attempted a forceful yank but the pressure was so intense it had me screaming as the shock ran through my body. I pulled, wriggled and fought desperately, contorting my body into all manner of strange shapes and positions. Still the boot showed no sign of budging. I swore constantly in a mixture of pain and frustration, I was nearly in tears. I tried again and the boot gave a slight movement, just enough to lever the toes of my good foot down the back of my heel. I pushed with everything I had, at the same time pulling the leg in the opposite direction with my hands clamped behind my knee. The boot moved like a live thing and flew off, landing a few metres away from me. My screams must have rung out across the entire valley.

'You fucking bastard,' I groaned as I slumped onto my back in utter exhaustion.

The relief was immediate and immeasurable as blood flowed back into my ankle and brought my foot back to life. The swelling subsided quickly and the pleasure was enough to cause me to let out a long sigh. My feet had felt comically huge, as if I was wearing oversized clown's shoes, now they seemed normal again. I went to work massaging more feeling back into both feet. The turnaround in my morale was incredible. Anger and frustration evaporated and for a few moments the satisfaction of being free of my boots and having warm, dry feet was indescribable. I remembered a passage from *Epitaph of a Small Winner* by Machado de Assis, a novel I had read recently: 'Tight boots are one of the greatest blessings in a man's life, because while they make your feet hurt, they also give rise to the pleasure of taking them off.'

Having dry socks and warm feet now motivated me to get organized. I awkwardly slid my legs inside the canoe sack and pulled it up as high as it would go. It was hardly a substitute for the sleeping bag, but would at least keep my feet and most of my legs dry, if not warm. For now it was a luxury.

I turned off my torch to save the batteries but the loss of light seemed to intensify the cold and loneliness. I was ravenously hungry so decided to eat something. Removing a frozen glove, I poured a handful of sausage roll crumbs into my palm, but my mouth was very dry, making it difficult to swallow. I took a swig of water and tried the cake crumbs, they were moist and soft and went down much more easily. It didn't occur to me how careless I had been until I put my hand into an empty bag, so much for conserving my supplies. For a few moments I felt the same shame I knew as a child after being caught out for a raid on the family goody box. It was an undisciplined mistake that could have dangerous consequences.

After fifteen minutes without the torchlight my eyes had become accustomed to the dark. Inactive and with nothing further to do, I had started to shiver again. I stared through the canopy, looking up into space. The moon gave out enough light for me to see the outline of trees and the black silhouette of the mountain top dominating the horizon. Stars floated and sparkled brilliantly. There was not even a whisper of a sound, nothing stirred in this frozen realm beneath the trees. The rest of the world and its people were somewhere distant and foreign, in a place that no longer existed for me. I was in my own exclusive space and time and there wasn't a person alive whose actions had any bearing on me. It was a rare thing indeed to be so divorced from everything else. In these moments, I struggled to contend with the idea that life as I knew it was still going on. I thought of my family at home, blissfully ignorant of my ordeal. Being so alone and far removed from everything I knew had a warping effect on my sense of reality. It was like the paradox of Schrödinger's cat, people and places couldn't exist again until I saw them, just as the cat was either alive or dead only upon opening the box and looking inside.

My mind eventually went quiet, soft thoughts of my family and comforting scenarios left me and I waited. Uncertain, unseeing and helpless to do anything, I was quickly overcome by a terrible sadness. There was nowhere for my mind or body to go, nothing to distract me and no task to apply myself to. Fear reactivated my mind and no matter how much I went over what had happened I couldn't imagine myself avoiding the avalanche or the fall. I began to wonder whether there existed some larger force operating beyond the power of my own free will, and that perhaps I didn't have a choice in my own fate after all. I didn't like to think so, but some feeling from within harangued me with the thought that all this was to teach me a lesson for coming to the mountain alone and for some of the bad things I had done in my life. Not knowing if I could get through the night was the worst part of it.

It's inevitable that when you sense death is coming, your life's entire history runs past your mind's eye. You suddenly find yourself with a lot of space and time to go over old memories. It's almost as if they're exhibits in a museum of your very own that you can pull out and inspect at will. The darkness seemed to bring my whole lifetime closer. I pulled my arms out from the sleeves and hugged them into my body, then ducked my head inside my jacket like a tortoise retreating into its shell. I hoped it would be enough to get me through to daylight. Early attempts to sleep were thwarted by discomfort and biting cold. Unable to escape from my troubled mind, anxiety stimulated my imagination, prompting nefarious visions and paranoid thoughts. Fear and uncertainty distorted all sense of time and place, intensifying my emotions. I could do nothing to fight it, the night was going to be a hellish waiting game. Even from the cocoon of my jacket the cold besieged me in a constant and cruel barrage. I knew that I wouldn't get any warmer as there was no way to revive any body heat without moving. Threatened by the savage temperature I realized I would probably die if I fell asleep. I resorted to repeating 'I mustn't sleep' over and over like a mantra.

Staving off the cold was only half the battle as I began to dwell heavily on the struggle that would ensue at first light. As much as I wanted and needed the morning to come, I dreaded its arrival in equal measure. My head was a maze of utter despair and confusion. Dangling dangerously on the verge of sleep, I tried to encourage fresh thoughts, even dark ones, anything to keep me awake. I had been this tired before on sentry duty and knew how seductive sleep could be. But in the army I'd always had someone to punch me awake if I fell asleep. Here I had no one, I was my own guardian. I had never imagined how hard it would be to find true strength;

everything before in my life had been a mere tester, a few foundation blocks in the process of character building.

Somehow holding onto a threadbare body temperature, I carried out a check on my symptoms: violent and uncontrollable shivering, an inability to think straight or pay attention, confusion, loss of judgment and reasoning, difficulty moving around, weakness, feeling afraid, slight memory loss, fumbling hands, slurred speech, slow, shallow breathing and a weak pulse. I was in a bad way but still had enough wits about me to read the signs and know I wasn't yet suffering from the later stages of hypothermia. More than anything the cold was spirit crushing. I simply had to endure it and fight the urge to sleep. When tiredness overcame me, it was never for more than a few seconds. I would doze off intermittently, only to be jerked back to consciousness by noises from the forest, falling rocks, small avalanches or the wind. Other times, I would wake in shock, unsure of the source of my disturbance, as though I had some sort of internal warning system that would sound an alarm to keep me alive.

As the night went on, my reactions and ability to think straight diminished. I repeatedly unzipped the neck of my jacket looking for a sign of daylight, desperate for it to be there, even though it would signal the start of the dreadful struggle I would have to make. The psychological trauma I inflicted upon myself was amazing, so much punishment and none of it serving any purpose. The entire night I played this cruel waiting game, pitting myself in a constant battle against sleep and the cold. I'd known many a beastly night sleeping in a hole in the ground, with my neck crooked and my feet aching with cold, but this was the longest night of my life.

CHAPTER FIVE

ESCAPE FROM THE MOUNTAIN

I emerged urgently from the shell of my jacket, unzipping the neck from the inside and worming my arms back into the sleeves. Issuing little puffs of steam from my mouth and nose, I watched as the pre-dawn glow lit up the silver sheen of frost and ice that covered the ground. Frozen branches above me sparkled like shards of glass, spilling a hazy flurry of ice and snow particles into the air. The early-morning chill needled my ears and the back of my neck as I watched the creeping line from the rising sun work its way down the mountain. If ever there was a frozen kingdom, this was it.

Still sitting in my canoe sack, I began looking around, breathing in the frigid air and trying to gather my confused thoughts. Distinctly lacking in any sort of objective and bereft of ideas, I felt hesitant and apprehensive about moving away from my safe spot. I started shouting for help for the first time since my fall, calling out as loudly as I was able.

Following each sequence of attempts I stopped to listen for a reply, but heard only echoes. I shouted for over an hour, my calls weakening as my voice faded, sometimes breaking into pathetic little sobs in between. But I had to keep at it knowing it might be my only chance. Between calls my mind played out various rescue scenarios. I imagined a helicopter hovering above the canopy, lowering a guide down to me on a rope, then being winched up and flown away wrapped in a woollen blanket, sipping hot, sweet tea. I had left a trace of my route with the receptionist at the hostel where I was staying and told her I would be back by late afternoon the next day or at the latest midday the following day. When I failed to return she would surely notify rescue or emergency services. In my mind I followed the line of detective enquiry: armed with a copy of my passport photo page the police would question all the taxi drivers at Fagaras. Who had driven me? What was the drop-off point? Did they have any other useful information? They would have tracker dogs and my calls would travel far across the landscape if the weather was still. Perhaps they would see the deep trail of my prints running up through the firebreak if the avalanche hadn't wiped the slope clean.

I couldn't convince myself of any of it and an anguished dread grew in my calls so I stopped yelling. The deadline I had given them would not be reached until late-afternoon today and even then, what if the receptionist forgot altogether or decided to leave it a few more hours before raising the alarm? And even if she did, no search team would come after dark. The realization was soul destroying, the prospect of another night out here in the wilderness even more so. Then a slight glimmer of hope came to me. I remembered that just after being dropped off by the taxi I had passed a young couple coming from the opposite direction down one of the hiking trails and we had exchanged greetings. At the time I'd been disappointed at encountering other people but now I was inspired by the possibility of hikers being out on the trails. I optimistically resumed my calls for help, holding out for as long as my vocal cords could take the strain. The process became automatic, requiring no thought or attention. It was strange listening to myself, as the longer I shouted 'help' the more the word lost its power and meaning. I was ashamed to find that it sounded as though I were crying wolf. The worst part of it was realizing the extent of my sheer desperation. In my life before I had always been able to bail myself out of difficult and dangerous situations, now I was begging for help. I had a lump in my throat and cried silently, like a scared child. At first, I tolerated my weakness in a sympathetic and understanding way, then became embarrassed. I was glad that nobody would ever see me in this state.

The stream at the bottom of the valley ran within a few kilometres of a footpath. I knew that if I could make it that far down I would have a chance. I could rest, rehydrate and my calls for help were more likely to be heard. Taking charge of myself, I was ready to put my plan into action. I removed my legs from the canoe sack, flexed my aching fingers and wriggled my toes to encourage some life back into my feet. Then I reached for my boots, they had frozen solid overnight and were coated with frost.

Squeezing the plastic lace head between a numb forefinger and thumb, I attempted to thread it through the eyeholes. Twenty minutes of effort ended in failure. Even with the Leatherman I couldn't breach a single hole. The top half of the boot had metal lace hangers secured from the ankle up, after failing miserably to lace them properly these hooks were now the best I could hope for. Remembering the trouble I had had removing them, I decided on my good leg first. The cold weather had frozen the insides and pulled the leather tight, causing the boot to shrink. I forced my foot in as hard as I could manage but the boot refused me entry, my heel progressing only slightly past the top band. The struggle was ominous. I knew these boots well having always relied on them for tough battle marches and daily duties. However, although they had survived an Arctic warfare course in Norway and hard marches in the Welsh mountains, they weren't ideal for the high mountains in winter. I really should have invested in a better pair. They were well broken-in and extremely comfortable, but they had a mind of their own and this wasn't the first time they had been so obstinate. On several occasions they had made me late for parade, causing me to be 'shelled', a physical punishment requiring the recipient to march with a deactivated artillery shell as an alternative to a monetary fine. I'd had enough difficulty with them in the past when I was in peak physical condition, now I had broken bones to contend with.

An hour-long struggle ensued, accompanied by expletives and sobs. I stretched the boots with my hands, breathed into them, and even attempted to heat their insides by holding them under my jacket pressed tight against my chest. When that didn't work, I tried to lever my foot in with a stick, while jamming the boot heel against a tree root. It was a ridiculous idea but I was desperate enough to try anything. Throughout the ordeal, I rolled, writhed and contorted my body in all manner of bizarre shapes and positions, demented with agony as my legs cramped and the broken bones moved. In the end I simply used my Leatherman blade to cut a slit down the back of the heel, but still the boot put up further resistance before it eventually allowed my foot in.

With the first boot back on, it then occurred to me I should have removed and replaced my dry sock with the wet one in my map pocket. It was bad drill not to follow the wet and dry routine but I would be damned if I was going

83

through that again. It had been hell and there was another one to go; the bad leg would be even worse. The struggle to put the boot on my left foot made the previous ordeal pale into insignificance. Even with the incision at the back, it came down to brute force. I might as well have been calling out for help as I screamed at the uncaring sky in a cacophony of agony induced noises which I never imagined I could make. The worst of it came at the end, my final push was too hard. A sharp crunch sounded as bone shifted up into my hip joint; the shock of it nearly caused me to pass out. Relieved, exhausted and triumphant I collapsed back onto the canoe sack. I decided I never wanted to go through that again, I would not remove the boots from now on.

After gathering my remaining items, I placed them into the canoe sack, rolled it tightly and clipped the ends together before tying the bundle into place with two lengths of para cord. With the roll secured onto my trouser belt loops I set off from behind the fallen trunk, heading immediately down slope. These first movements were slow and painful; my body was stiff and extremely cold. I thought about the night and the memory turned on fear like a light switch. I had to get moving, reasoning that the more ground I covered, the greater my chances of being found. I genuinely worried another night exposed in the open would kill me.

The ground changed constantly as I made my way down

slope, shifting between beds of snow, bare rock and dense layers of frost that whispered a crack as it caught the early morning sun. Many of the flat-faced rocks were covered in thin veins of ice displaying different colours depending on the nature of the stone beneath. Others sparkled like crystal where thick tear-shaped icicles had formed from freezing water. I ploughed my way through deep drifts of fresh powder snow that squeaked as I passed over it, sinking in as I went. Older snow was more compact and easier to move across, making more of a crunching sound as I broke the hard crust that had frozen overnight. Where the tree canopy was dense there were exposed areas of forest litter, mostly old branches and twigs that had come down as deadfall, bringing the occasional bird's nest with it. Gentle wave-like drifts of pine needles that changed in colour according to their age formed over lumpy mounds of soil.

I quickly discovered how much easier it was going down than it had been going up, it just required skill and concentration to control my injured leg. Before each slide forward, I firmly dug my boot heel into the earth, assisting the rest of the movement with my arms. On difficult and steep stretches, I wedged my boot against a tree or rock to be sure I wasn't sent tumbling down again. It didn't take long until my advance became a series of rehearsed and well-drilled movements with strict adaptations for each obstacle encountered.

Using an array of rolls, shuffles, levers and various slides, I was able to negotiate everything the forest floor put in my way. It impressed me how my body could compensate and adapt. Occasionally, my canoe sack became an obstruction, interrupting my tempo by dragging behind me, or getting snagged on undergrowth and bits of broken branch. For as long as the ground allowed me to slide along on my ass, I would sit it on my lap and clip it to my front belt loops. When I switched back onto my stomach, I would attach it behind me again.

I checked my watch for the first time that morning: it was 11 o'clock. It felt like I had been moving for ever but it had only been ninety minutes. Time seemed to move as slowly as I did and knowing how much further I had to go only added to my mental trauma. As the day went on I slowed dramatically and became increasingly cold. I tried to hurry my pace, but my ability to coordinate myself had severely diminished. I became increasingly clumsy and banged and twisted my leg with greater frequency, initiating bursts of white-hot pain, accompanied by the grisly noise of moving bones. I was creeping along, as aware of the enormous variations in ground as a small animal might be. Before long I was moving only by inertia, I couldn't believe how quickly everything had fallen apart. With no way to combat the fatigue, I used any movement I was capable of to get my body down the slope. I was cold, tired, hungry and thirsty, the inside of my mouth was rigid, horribly dry and tasted disgusting. Each time I came to a stop, sleep beckoned and my eyelids began to droop. The pain in my leg got worse and the combined effect of it all made me wonder if I had breached a physical limit beyond which I had nothing more to give. I was ready to quit; some defeated part of my mind deciding I had had enough. Slumping to the ground I lay still, refusing my body the liberty of movement. It made no difference how fast or slow I moved, I realized I would still be spending another night somewhere under these trees. Nobody was coming for me until tomorrow at the earliest.

Although something inside urged me to keep going, I remained stubborn. I tried to pretend I was stopping for a rest – it was a lie, I was ready to stop for good. My ability was no longer equal to my earlier ambitions, and the discipline to suppress my defeated thoughts had disappeared.

I was drifting into a sleep when something kicked in me. It was as if there was some level of my consciousness constantly overcoming the lower, weaker part of myself that wanted to give up or take rest. It was always operating: making plans, sounding alarms and setting commands, ever ready to wake me from any state detrimental to my survival. I knew that staying put wasn't an option. I was beyond the reach of help and if I stopped my progress I'd only be delaying the inevitable. I turned my body and began ploughing a route directly down the slope. For at least thirty minutes my motion was constant, I tried to go on for longer but it had turned into a fight for air. Uninterrupted crawling was an exhausting endeavour, only sustainable for a limited time. Keeping my head down, I would look up every so often to make sure I was following a straight line. I allowed myself ten seconds of rest for every ten drags forward I achieved. It was a workable pace and keeping count kept my mind busy and the rest breaks enticed me onward as if they were some great reward. Another hour passed, I must have dragged myself for just under a kilometre. My body was adapting well to its workload and able to overcome everything except the worst attacks of pain. When I started to waver, I tried to encourage a response by muttering more old army aphorisms.

'Don't jack! Pain is merely weakness leaving the body.'

It had been the company pill, yet such simple words remained strangely potent after many years.

After being on the ground for so many hours, I became gripped with curiosity to know what lay ahead. All this time I had felt so small in comparison to the daunting landscape. Moving at a snail's pace, even the smallest distances appeared vast. At the next stop I used a large rock to pull myself up onto one shaky leg. Scanning the ground ahead, I looked for an easy route down and a definite point to aim for. The slope disappeared into dead ground a couple of hundred metres ahead of me. Still, this was the furthest I had been able to see in any direction. I pivoted 180° to look back up the mountain, studying the tracks of the bizarre meandering route I had actually taken. I thought I had been going in a straight line, the zigzagged trail cut into the snow and earth told another story.

My routine of ten drags to ten seconds rest ended just after midday. By this stage my breaks were becoming longer and more frequent. I tried to impose other, more manageable goals, and forced myself not to fret about the distance. If I could reach the stream, that would be it, anything further in my state was unthinkable. I promised to commit to a solid thirty-minute block of crawling, then I would allow myself a real rest; I gave it everything I had and lasted another hour. By 2.30 I was too exhausted to think or count and only moved when I could. I was becoming detached, zombie-like and uncaring. Actions and movements became a blur, my mind devoid of thoughts and my body free from pain and cold. I became lost. There were long stretches of crawling where I recalled absolutely nothing.

Time passed and the shadows grew longer. By three o'clock I had become a complete physical wreck. Although there were fewer than two hours daylight remaining I needed a more substantial break, so stopped at the next suitable place. At rest, my attention was drawn to the blood around my wrists. I sat upright, rolled up my sleeves and removed both gloves. Hundreds of black pine needles and slivers of wood were embedded in my fingers and palms. I had to wipe away the blood to see the full extent of the damage. I wished I hadn't looked. As with the wounds elsewhere on my body, I was probably better off not knowing. By now I was crying out for sleep more than ever, my chin sagged onto my chest and my eyelids flickered uncontrollably. I had reached the stage where I couldn't lie down or lean against a tree during a rest stop without falling asleep. Keeping my back upright and un-supported was the only way to combat it. It was only my thirst that encouraged me to get going again; calling for help was relegated to a distant second place. I constantly imagined the taste of cool water running over my cracked lips and through my parched mouth. I tried to swallow but my throat felt as though I had swallowed sand and my tongue was so dry it was sticking to the roof of my mouth. I contorted my cheek muscles to encourage saliva but it was like getting blood from a stone. I put my gloves back on and set off. At my next time check the area in front of me opened up, offering a good line of sight for a couple of hundred metres and allowing light to pour through the trees in wider beams. The most encour-aging sign was the profile of the slope; it had panned out, giving promise that I was close to the bottom. Although normal time and distance scales meant nothing, I tried to estimate how far I had come. I guessed it to be around 2 kilometres. Emboldened, I told myself that with one more big effort I'd reach the stream.

At the next patch of snow, I stopped to scoop up a small handful and put it in my mouth. It refused to melt and sent a cold shock through my back teeth. I stayed for five minutes, feeding myself sugar-cube-sized lumps. It did little to alleviate my thirst but temporarily soothed the insides of my dry mouth. Inspired by my desire for a real drink, I got going again. I had only covered another 100 metres when my arms buckled under my weight. Crossing the flat belt quickly turned into a nightmare, the ground was a minefield of forest debris and rock that had tumbled down the mountainside and accumulated at the bottom. The effect on my morale of getting ready to withstand each new bout of crawling was devastating. I was weakening quickly, one collapse was followed shortly by another, snowballing into consecutive breakdowns. It frightened me how rapidly I could see-saw between a state of readiness and feeling totally done in. I still fought with everything I had to keep myself moving, but the distance between my bursts of activity was coming down rapidly: five body lengths and drop, three body lengths . . . two . . . and then immediate collapse. I was going nowhere. Flattened by the urge to sleep I lay still and closed my eyes.

I woke startled and confused. I nearly fell back into a leaden unconsciousness, but managed to pull myself upright. My vision was out of focus and my head ached from the effects of sheer exhaustion and dehydration. I looked around trying to take in the surroundings just to reaffirm my situation. How long had I been out for? I checked my watch, what felt like hours had been only five minutes. I wanted to feel guilty for wasting time, but initially lacked the focus to care. I tried to shock myself into wakefulness with a pretence of rage and even then it took a few minutes to rally my body into moving again. After each stop restarting was like getting the engine of an old car going; it needed a lot of encouraging. As I began assessing a probable route through the trees, I realized I was disoriented. The ground was pan flat with no distinguishable features and no snow tracks to follow. It was a bad sign that I could so easily lose my bearings; sleep had blunted my instinct and directional awareness. I used the compass to correct my direction and got under way.

The effort I was asking of my muscles became too much in less than five minutes. Something would give way every 10 to 20 metres, leaving me totally incapable of lifting myself until my arms had recovered. To get going again I became totally subordinate to the mantras and commands I continued to address to myself. It was like the Royal Air Force dispatcher's order to jump on the green light. 'Green on . . . Go!' Followed by a forceful shove on the shoulder, out the door and into the slipstream. 'One thousand, two thousand, three thousand, check canopy.'

I depended on these orders as an antidote to my trepidation. In the army I'd always had backup and it wasn't as though introspection had much freedom or space to flourish, the bravado of the group kept many of our private fears at bay. Alone in this desolate place it was easier to recognize fear in myself and there was no place to hide from it. I was strong and fit and probably in the best shape of my life. My body had carried me all over the world and through a lifetime of sporting and physical challenges. I was rarely ill and my physical strength and endurance were part of my very identity. Now my body was failing me and I was scared. Never before had I felt so strongly overcome by a sense of danger and my own vulnerability. To be so powerless was to know sheer desolation. Fear of the unknown can have the most devastating effects. With my physical capabilities fading, cracks started to appear in my mental resilience. The shame I felt at wanting to give up drove me on even though I was being worn down with shocking speed. Yet the amount of pain I could stand kept on expanding, stretching like elastic.

My attention shifted back to the terrain and the unwanted discovery that the ground began to gradually drop away once more. I wasn't at the bottom after all, which meant the stream could still be a long way off. Facing the night without water was too much, all that crawling for a drink thwarted by some small distance I was unable to cover. I rolled onto my backside and sat up. A few moments to focus and I was off again. I kept telling myself I would be all right, it was just mental. Always when I was at my lowest ebb, some shift in conditions, physical or geographic, could adjust my mental state, arousing emotions of anger, sadness or determination. Like a small spark, it would ignite something in me, just enough to get me going again, to push me on when I felt I had no more to give. My body was compensating well considering the massive task it was undertaking, maybe I had more in me than I imagined. That's the thing with perceived limits – you never really know how much you have left in the tank. All in the head, I reminded myself.

I checked my watch again and looked up at the sky. There was little left of the day. I began bombing my way down, sledging over the snow, with my bad leg crossed over the other, braking with my hands and boot heel. Where the slope was steep enough I would slide, anywhere else I shuffled like a madman, trying to drop as much height as possible. I was gasping for breath and the sweat began to trickle down my spine under the layers of my clothes. My hard work left me disappointed that this surge in effort hadn't come earlier. Dusk was spreading over the forest floor and a slight wind picked up as the light faded, making strange noises through the trees. Convinced I'd heard water, I dropped down another 20 metres to stop and listen. I couldn't hear anything over the sound of my own heavy laboured breathing. I waited for my racing pulse and heart to slow down. Nothing . . . perhaps I'd been tricked by the wind. Still convinced I was on the verge of making it, I moved and shuffled my way down like crazy, smashing and catching my leg so many times that the pain just merged into one constant block of agony. When I thought I heard the sound of flowing water again, I laughed greedily and sent myself hurtling down the slope. My state was frantic and my cognitive skills reduced to ash. At the edge of a steep section, the ground dropped away suddenly, loose soil gave way beneath an outstretched arm and the rest of my body followed. As I tumbled my jaw took a heavy impact against a rock and I came to a stop. I lay stunned and barely conscious as stars circled my head. I could no longer hear the blissful sound of running water, only the whining howl of the wind. I lay back, shut my eyes and waited for my head to clear.

CHAPTER SIX

SECOND NIGHT IN THE OPEN

When I woke it was dark, the night was upon me and with it my worst fears. I tried to hold on to the light of the stars that had kept me company through many a bad night in my life before. The cold and pain were just mere factors I could choose to cope with or not, it was the sheer emptiness and uncertainty of waiting that got to me most. Looking back up at the sky for inspiration, I felt a frozen tear on my cheek. I'd never felt so completely alone in my entire life. Valueless questions whirled in my head before giving way to warmer thoughts. I remembered playing football with my brother for our awful pub team – some of the happiest memories of my life. The distance from home seemed inconceivably far and I just couldn't escape the feeling of being totally out of reach.

Sitting in the dark, dwelling on the sheer horror of my situation, an utter helplessness resounded throughout every corner of my mind, causing tension to flow through my body, pulling my chest tight and sending out a dull ache that I could feel in every organ, nerve, muscle and bone. But the thing about the shock and emotion you feel in extreme circumstances is that the initial impact grips you and reaches almost unimaginable heights before eventually having to let you go. And after, it doesn't feel so bad, the mind stabilizes, returns to survival mode and begins to function again. Before you know it, there is a shred of hope and you can start to believe.

The plummeting temperature rudely interrupted my sorrowful state and knocked some sense back into me. It served as a harsh reminder that this was far more than a mental battle. I had to prepare to get through the night. I moved my body around my injured leg in a series of cautious, short, circular movements, until my legs were inside the canoe sack. This time, I didn't remove my boots. I went into my tortoise procedure, tucking my head and arms inside my jacket and hugging them into my body. It took ages to regenerate some body heat, and even when I did, I was still freezing. The night was no different from the previous one: sleepless, bone-chillingly cold and spent in constant anticipation of daylight. I summoned all my energy and focus into maintaining a high state of alertness and waited. The wind howled without let, blowing against my body and the canoe sack, making an irritating kite-like flapping sound. I shivered uncontrollably in my shell and wondered if it was physically possible to feel any colder.

As the night went on the symphony of the forest opened up: the clatter of falling rocks and distant roar of avalanches travelled fast and far from the upper slopes and an evil wind blew down from further up the valley and sighed among the crevices of the mountain. The darkness brought my senses alive and I began to hear and sense a presence that sickened me with fear. I felt watched and convinced myself that a pack of wolves, drawn by the smell of my blood were scenting the air and homing in on me through the trees. The idea of being eaten alive overtook me, an act of self-deception so strong that I withdrew from my jacket to keep watch. Within seconds, I lost valuable body heat to the stabbing cold air, sending me into heavy and uncontrollable shivers, with any part of me directly exposed burning with cold. I pulled my hat down as far as it would go and my collar up and stared out into the coal-black night, standing guard for invisible horrors. I waited for over an hour, holding a small rock and my Leatherman, ready to bludgeon or stab anything that came near. The darkness seemed to hang over me like some spectre watching and waiting for its chance to take me. The fear was so intense I felt sick to my stomach. I'd never known torment, real or imagined, like it. It was all pure imagination but it felt real enough at the time. I made solemn and determined promises not to drift into a fatal sleep as though to do so was a deliberate action.

Eventually I summoned up the courage to drop my guard and re-establish my tortoise procedure. Although my resistance to sleep was sincere enough, I couldn't trust myself to maintain sufficient discipline to remain inside my jacket. I had never waited for dawn with such desperation, and in spite of the blackness of the sky, I repeatedly and treacherously unzipped my collar to see if daylight had arrived. Gambling away precious body heat was a risk I was willing to take. Only once did I look at my watch, the luminous hands read midnight. Time had never moved so slowly. Yet, despite the horrors of what had passed, when the dawn broke behind the mountaintops and the first narrow streaks of pink and gold touched the sky, the nightmares seemed less solid and everything resumed its normal proportions. I was still alive and had survived another night.

CHAPTER SEVEN

BETWEEN THE WOODS AND THE WATER

My first movements of the day were slow and frozen. I sat up and stared vacantly down the slope in a blurred delirium, looking at nothing and somehow trying to work out if all this was real. It was hard, almost impossible to believe, but my cold aching body reminded me how true it all was. I knew what I was in for so felt some apprehension about the dreaded prospect of dragging myself down the slope. For some time I just sat and watched my breath projecting long thin streams of vapour which rose and then vanished into the icy air. Eventually, after issuing myself with a stern order I rolled my canoe sack back up and checked that I had all my remaining equipment, that all buttons were fastened and zips done up before selecting a rough route and moving off. With the strengthening light, I began to feel remarkably energized and positive. I'd always loved mountains for the sense of the spectacular they offered, but this morning was a gift appreciated as never before. As a complete mental and physical turnaround dramatically came over me, I was able to comprehend all I had been through on the mountain. A lot had been thrown at me, yet I was still going. After warming up, I was moving so efficiently that I hardly noticed my left leg was badly smashed. I received frequent sharp and painful reminders of its sorry state, but was determined not to let it interfere with my momentum. Inspired by the idea that my efforts would be rewarded, I pushed, pulled and lowered myself down the slope with everything I had to give. After the night, I was determined to put every second of daylight to use. Both my body and mind fell into a zone dedicated only to movement, devoid of all thought, immune to the cold and able to resist almost any pain.

It was well past ten o'clock when I made my first real stop. I had crawled without let for nearly three hours and had reached a point where I could no longer go on unless I had a break. I took a rest for close to fifteen minutes even though I hadn't intended it to be so long. Watching the second hand move round my watch dial, I kept promising myself another minute, one after another. I set off again but it wasn't long before I was breathing heavily and the pain made its customary return. Within a couple of hundred metres, I started to notice a slight delay in the synchronicity between mental commands and my actual movements. It was as though the mechanics of my body were beginning to fail. I couldn't identify one area of pain or cold from the other, everything either hurt or was frozen. I was falling apart just as suddenly as I had experienced my earlier surge of power; the revival was coming to an end. I found a tree to rest against and tried to recover my breath. I began repeating a line I liked from the film *Trainspotting*: 'It's a shite state of affairs to be in, Tommy, and all the fresh air in the world won't make any fucking difference.'

The line pleased me immensely; I laughed out loud and said it again. When I tired of it, I sat in silence and another fifteen minutes passed.

A recurring procession of nonsense ran through my mind: discouraging thoughts, ideas of rest and a parade of fairy-tale rescue scenarios. I knew I had to maintain a constant vigil or my mind would drift into its own world, oblivious to my troubles and embracing sleep, but the awareness of this danger didn't stop it happening or make it any easier to get going again after each period of rest.

Bitterly cold from my prolonged stop, I was shivering and shaking. The frost my breath had made stuck to the high collar of my jacket, which I had pulled up to the bridge of my nose, and my teeth were beginning to chatter. My hands and feet felt like stone and my toes were devoid of all sensation. Although the pain had lessened in my leg, I could barely reach beyond my knees, a sure sign that the joint was beginning to fuse. Starting to move my stiff limbs again required a huge effort, but the desire for water propelled me forward. In my zeal and confusion, I set off in the wrong direction but realized my mistake quickly and adjusted my course. Following a sustained thirty-minute effort the gradient of the slope began to level off and the topography gradually changed. Especially welcome was the open canopy, which let in more light and encouraged patches of vegetation on the forest floor. I came to a stop and looked skywards. The clouds were heavy and white, it would likely snow again. Relieved to have left the miserable slope behind, I felt sure I had reached the bottom of the mountain proper and couldn't be too far from the stream, maybe within a hundred metres given that the valley floor was quite narrow. In spite of being so near it wasn't long before my arms gave way and I dropped flat on the side of my face again. I wasn't sure if it was fatigue or a weak mind. Over the last hour I'd been looking for any old excuse to stop and take a break. Leg pain was often my justification; this time it was frozen feet. The condition of my body yo-yoed with startling frequency, just as my mind hovered between the gloomiest pessimism and wildest optimism. Whenever I suffered such lapses, I would bully myself with strict orders and try to re-assert all the tough-guy philosophies from my years in the army. It was a single-minded and one-dimensional form of determination: when I gave myself an order, I usually obeyed. Old habits die hard and when the going got really tough it all kicked in again, forcing me into making decisions and quickly eradicating any doubts, emerging weaknesses or unsoldierly thoughts. A flood of army experiences ran through my mind like a film, their memory reviving my energy and will to overcome anything. I wondered if I could have survived up until now without my training.

I set off again, armed with inexorable, aggressive and obstinate tenacity. I was back on my belt buckle, dragging and crawling with everything I could physically muster. I began designating targets a short distance ahead, which I had to reach without stopping or looking up. Covering ground in these manageable splits worked for a good while, and I expected to see or hear water at any moment. Despite my efforts each new horizon was the same, trees and flat snow-covered ground, beds of pine needles and the occasional patch of vegetation. I was soon panting for breath and my back was soaked in sweat, which would freeze every time I dropped to my belly. The effects of my charged state soon began to wear off and despite my commands, my arms would quickly turn to jelly and give way, sometimes collapsing immediately after restarting. Unable to persevere, I had to take lengthy and regular rests.

Reduced to crawling on my elbows, I dragged myself

until all my basic systems of movement failed. I crumpled in a heap and remained there, unable to raise my chest off the ground for more than a few seconds. Resenting my body's weakness, I shouted desperately at my arms – for a moment experiencing welcome catharsis – then diverted my attention to my injured leg and became furious. After swearing savagely I came close to tears. I didn't know why, perhaps it was loneliness more than frustration. I thought about my family and felt a terrible sadness that I would never see them again. My heart ached with loneliness and I started to cry. When I pulled myself together I felt embarrassed at yet another theatrical performance. Even though there was no one to hear me complain or cry, I imagined people I knew disapproving of my feebleness. I had thought I was tougher than this. After a lengthy recovery and much self-pity, I was able to get up and start moving again, covering around a hundred metres in less than five minutes without stopping. I rested briefly and continued dragging myself until I reached a pocket of deep snow. I crawled across its crunchy surface for a further 20 metres before being stopped by the blissful sound of water. Enlivened, I gauged the rough direction of the source and lunged forward, obsessed with quenching a thirst that consumed me.

Sitting on the bank, I watched the flow of the stream, scanning along the side for an access point. The water was deep and out of my reach from the high vertical edges of its bank.

I considered leaning out head first, but realized I would never reach, or worse, I would slip and plunge into the ice-cold water. The idea came to me that I could fish some water out with my plastic water bottle, all I needed was a line. Rummaging through my pockets I searched out my bootlaces and joined them together to make one length. Endeavours to tie the lace around the neck of the bottle were slow and clumsy, hindered by my numb fingers. I blew air into my cupped hands until they had warmed enough for me to complete the job, wrapping the other end of the lace around my palm to ensure I didn't lose the bottle.

I shuffled forward a few inches until safely positioned at the edge of the bank before lowering myself to a prone position, my arm hanging down towards the water. I had fancied it would come gushing into the bottle but the result left me disappointed. The container bobbed up and down on the surface as the flow carried it downstream, pulling the line taut against my hand. Nothing more than a few drops sat at the bottom. I reeled out some more lace from my hand, allowing the bottle to be taken further downstream. In a controlled motion I pulled it back towards me, the action forcing the nose of the bottle under the surface, catching over an inch of water. I repeated the process, gaining the same amount again. The third pull was unsuccessful, spilling as much as I had gained. I tried again, learning that two pulls obtained the optimum amount of water the bottle could hold without losing any. Satisfied, I reeled it back in, and brought it to my lips. A chilling shock ran through my back teeth, causing me to splutter and choke, losing most of the water across my face and down my neck. Next time I would sit up straight: drinking on my stomach hadn't been the most sensible position. Urgently, I sent the line out again and reeled in another 4 centimetres of water, the relief to my parched mouth was instant and every bit as soothing as I had imagined. I drained the last drop before manically returning the bottle to the stream. My mouth was dry again before I had completed a refill.

The next hour became a frenzied blur of uninterrupted drinking and fishing for water. With every drop I could feel my strength slowly returning, the dryness in my throat and mouth was gone, my headache subsided and new levels of energy seemed to flow through my body. When I thought I had drunk all I could, the urge for more quickly returned. I kept going until my stomach was bloated and my body felt like a saturated sponge. Watching the water move, I rolled onto my side and took a piss, by the time I was done I was caught in the soothing pull of the stream's current. I slumped back against a tree with my arms folded across my belly. Feeling as though I had all the time in the world, I felt reluctant to move and disturb my moment's peace. My mind took off and began to fly, soaring through the clouds and over distant and exotic lands. I relived flashes of events on the mountain, from the fall to reaching water and everything in between. It was still very much happening, yet it all felt so distant, almost as if it never really was. I was in a state of luxurious indifference, all I wanted to do was shut off my thoughts and sleep, and for some time I did just that.

I awoke with a start, oblivious to how much time had passed. The sleep still in my eyes had frozen and become elastic and sticky like gum. I wet the end of my sleeve and wiped my face, lifting off a filthy mixture of blood, snot and dirt that had congealed into my eyelashes and three days of beard growth. I'd once been six weeks in the Brunei jungle with only one real wash in a river, so dirt never worried me. In a guilt-propelled hurry at having dozed off, I pulled my map out and tried to figure out what I would do from here on. A footpath ran through the forest on the other side of the stream. The nearest point was just over a kilometre away. A kilometre and a half or so beyond that was a vehicle track, the principal route in for farmers, loggers and hopefully mountain rescue. If I could reach it and someone drove by, I would be saved. Regardless of the massive distance involved, I began to believe I could make it to my new objective, it was all downhill with the route channelling me to the confines of the valley. I just had to keep crawling.

Before setting off I ate some of the sausage roll crumbs

and drank a further two inches of water before making a final refill. With the stream to guide me I no longer needed the map to navigate so folded it away and returned it to its pocket. Improvising a new technique of moving, I rolled over onto one knee, with palms flat on the ground, and assumed a three-legged table position. To move, I reached forward one hand at a time and brought my good knee in towards me, carrying out a sort of one-legged baby crawl. The first attempts at the new manoeuvre were awkward and painful, requiring patience and good balance. After a good test run, I found it to be the easiest and most energy efficient way of moving so far.

I shuffled my way down the valley with a steady rhythm; having the stream in such close proximity gave me extra reassurance. As I dropped height, the forest opened up and allowed in glorious amounts of light compared to the darkness of higher ground and the landscape also took on subtle changes. Whereas the terrain on the slopes consisted of uniform beds of snow, earth and pine needles, both sides of the water now presented rock formations, cliffs and small scree slopes. With the refreshing shift in scenery I felt calm and capable, my will to keep moving had been regenerated by a genuine belief that the worst was over. To keep up my motivation I relied on playing a game of beating the clock: I would pick a spot and give myself varying increments of time to get there. Breaking my journey down into these manageable legs helped me concentrate entirely on my immediate objective.

After a while, I developed astonishingly accurate time-distance estimations. Beating the clock urged me on, and when I had more than a minute to spare I was jubilant. If I failed, I felt dejected and ashamed, knowing that each defeat was part of something bigger. For each occasion I didn't make it I demanded of myself that I would take a minute off the next leg. Knocking off extra seconds involved a monstrous exertion, leaving me collapsed in a heap and fighting frantic-ally for breath. The game was good for a few hours before my earlier efforts caught up with me. Being unable to keep within my time schedules was only the start of my deterior-ation. As I became more incapable, I continually forgot the time I was supposed to achieve and the game lost its purpose. I had returned to the state I was so familiar with, one of com-plete and utter physical and mental destruction. Though I was still moving, distances and speeds were unregulated and unscheduled. While I struggled to contend with ideas of rest, the strong martial voice of reason would rescue me from my stupor, issuing commands I knew I had to obey. A distinct pattern was starting to emerge in my cycles of movement and energy levels. There were always ups and downs, mostly from one extreme to the other. The key to getting through the physical breakdowns was psychological; retaining some control over my mind was the difference between making it and not. I had to stay focused, be patient and accept rest when it was needed.

The next thing I knew, I saw that my way was blocked. I looked around for some other landmark that offered me the possibility of a way through and pointlessly studied the map, already knowing there were no alternatives. I had simply run out of track and space and was going to have to cross the stream. Instead of moving, I remained on the bank, staring dispassionately down into the transparent water, losing myself in the flow of ripples and small currents, following them downstream until they met with the crystal-like display of icicles formed on the overhanging foliage. The slope on my side of the stream merged into a high section of rock and boulders, dropping off sharply and turning into an impassable cliff. The stream narrowly contoured the bottom of the high sided grey wall, leaving me with no room to get through. I thought about backtracking to look for a passage up slope, but the distance was unknown and finding a route to box round the cliff would be a matter of chance. It was hardly worth contemplating. I no longer possessed the strength to drag myself back up the slope. I could barely manage on flat ground.

I estimated the water's depth to be about waist height. I had been able to crawl up to this point with a broken leg using a hastily devised repertoire of techniques and movements, but I couldn't imagine how I would get to the other side of the stream on one leg. If I slipped and submerged, my jacket would never dry and I would die within the hour. It would have provided a tricky and dangerous challenge for a fit and able-bodied person, what chance did I have in such ice-cold conditions? I was doomed. It saddened me that I had come all this way only to come unstuck here. Shaking from the cold and still undecided, I remained at the water's edge. It was essentially a wild gamble, I had only to cross a stream less than 3 metres wide, yet one small mistake or a slip and I would perish. If I stayed here and did nothing, I would meet the same fate. It was a similar predicament to the search for my sleeping bag: stagnation or suicide. I racked my brains for a plan and ideas came aplenty, but they were mostly absurdly stupid ones. The obvious one was to build a bridge, so I rummaged around the immediate area looking for any fallen branches that would hold my weight. All I came across were rocks, which gave rise to my most ridiculous initiative, that of damming the stream. I quickly realized it would only displace the water level, making the stream an even more fearsome barrier, and that even if I had the time to construct a dam, most of the stones were too heavy for me to move.

Devising these ridiculous river crossing strategies temporarily distracted me from my earlier fears and somehow made the task less daunting. I crawled back up stream until I reached a sharp bend I had passed not long before. The natural curve had almost formed an island of the opposite bank, making a narrower crossing site. Nearby, I found a strong-looking stick to aid my balance. I tested my weight on it to make sure it would be up to the job. It bowed slightly but didn't break. Confident it could bear my weight, I shuffled forward so that my ass sat on the edge of the bank and hung my legs down into the water. I remained in that position for some time, making excuses and inviting reasons to delay any action. I even started shouting for help, a cowardly attempt to delay the inevitable. The situation reminded me of my childhood fear of jumping from the high diving board at the local swimming pool. The moments of hesitation before I dived had been full of fear and dread, getting worse each time I returned to the back of the line. Jumping was never actually that bad, it was just the waiting and build-up of anxiety that made me suffer. I was simply concerned about the sensation before having experienced the effect. The analogy made me realize this turmoil was unnecessary and self-induced, so I wasted no more time. Not wanting to risk both my layers – my jacket and thermal vest – in one throw, I removed them one at a time and launched them across the water. My canoe sack was supposed to serve as a flotation device as well as keeping items dry, but was now full of holes from being dragged behind me over the treacherous mountain terrain.

With my jacket now hanging from a branch on the opposite side of the stream, I was beginning to feel the effects of cold across my naked torso. Like a nervous swimmer at the poolside, I cautiously lowered myself, breathing sharply as the icy water inched its way up my thighs. With only one working leg, I relied on the bank to keep stable while I waited for my body to adjust to the freezing temperature. I had an early scare when my injured leg, which floated uselessly, was snatched away by the pull of the current. To make sure it didn't happen again I carefully allowed my boot to rest on the bottom without bearing any weight, anchoring it against the pull of the stream. With my balance regained, I turned slowly, facing the way I had come with both arms fixed to the bank. Inch by inch, I wriggled my good boot against the stones on the stream bed, shuffling backwards and further out into the water. My movements were so nervous and minimal that after ten minutes, I had gained the distance of only one arm's length and even that had required fierce concentration. I was so cold that I started to shake uncontrollably. The skin on my upper body had turned red, then purple and was soon covered in goose bumps. I looked like a plucked turkey.

Now that I was more than an arm's length away from the bank and the support it offered me I had to turn and face my intended direction. Moving through 180° was slow and tricky, requiring many minute adjustments as I pivoted on my toes. At the end of the manoeuvre, I steadily let go of the side and brought my arms back into my body. I was now standing on one leg in the middle of the stream, relying only on the staff for support. I became momentarily fixed to the spot, without an idea of what to do next and unable to think how I would get my good leg forward. It took a blast of cold air to force me into a decision. There was no way round it, I was going to have to allow weight to bear on my injured leg. I reached my left arm slightly in front and planted the staff firmly into the stream bed, giving it a forceful twist to prevent it from slipping. I put some weight through it to make sure, then coaxed my bad leg forward, bringing it level with the staff. I knew from the boot-removal experience that if I bent the knee I could direct some pressure away from my broken bones. If I got on tiptoes, I hoped the ankle and knee would act as shock absorbers just long enough for me to do something with my working leg.

The first attempt ended with a bolt of incandescent pain. I hadn't put enough weight through the staff so I tried again, this time distributing more tension onto the stick. I took a deep breath, held it in and made the slightest hop forward. It was my first real advance even though it couldn't have been more than a couple of centimetres. As soon as I had fully regained my balance, I transferred all the pressure back onto my good leg and braced myself to try again. It took around ten more repeats to draw both legs level, and by the time I had repeated the action I had been in the water thirty minutes. I had covered the equivalent of two normal steps in distance. Seeing me in action must have been like watching a plant grow. It was demoralizing to learn that a successful crossing would involve agonizingly inching my way across. The only relief was that the freezing temperatures had lessened the pang of leg pain, anaesthetizing my nerve endings and preventing cramp from setting in.

As I progressed the depth of the water increased. I could feel the gradual creep of water rising up my legs, past my waist and eventually reaching my belly button. Each rise caused me to breathe in sharply, my teeth started chattering and my balls ached horribly, feeling as if they had turned to ice. My feet, which had felt like stumps before I entered the water, now felt as though they were warming up. I knew this wasn't a good sign. With the increase in depth, my already tightrope-like balance was becoming even more precarious. At the midway point, the current took my leg away again. The counter-move to regain my balance left me facing the wrong direction and once again stuck to the spot. I had to fight to keep vertical by leaning into the flow of the water, tensing my stomach muscles, bending at the knee and spreading out my arms just over the surface. The thought of going under made me shudder. I forced a risky manoeuvre to adjust my footing, spinning my body 45° so that I was again facing the other side of the stream. I relied on nothing other than luck and support from the stick, that I managed to avoid going in was nothing short of miraculous.

The strain of maintaining non-stop concentration momentarily eclipsed all else. As I came closer to the far side, shallower waters made my balancing act easier, but resisting the temptation to make a lunge wasn't so simple. Only when I was within reach of the side did I let go of the staff and allow my arms to take my weight. With a firm hold, I edged a little closer and made two mad hops on my good leg before throwing my arms over the side and sluggishly pulling myself out. It had taken me one hour to cross. At first I couldn't think or act, a shock-induced delay followed before I remembered my jacket. I crawled over to the tree and freed it from the branch. Before putting it back on, I rolled around in the snow to absorb the wetness from my drenched trousers. Fortunately, I had decided to wear my army-issue jungle trousers, hardly ideal mountain wear, but they were thin, lightweight and retained very little water. Having my jacket back on quickly raised some heat into my upper body, though not enough to avoid the onset of hypothermia. To prevent my condition from degenerating I had to get going. Despite my rapid deterioration, crossing the stream had buoyed my confidence. I could hardly believe that I had made it and now felt that the mountain could throw nothing worse at me. Being on the other side gave me a sense of security, it was as though I had escaped the clutches of a cruel and unforgiving landscape.

I followed the stream closely for the next thirty minutes before the ground started to rise steeply. The incline was only gradual, but quickly took its toll. Halfway up I considered discarding my canoe sack as it had become a nuisance dragging behind me after one of my rear belt loops had torn. I decided against it, convinced it would have some further use. Crawling uphill got my circulation going again so that now only my feet and hands were cold. Once at the top, my position allowed me to see what I would have been up against on the other side: the cliff was steep, high and unbroken. I wouldn't have stood a chance. After dropping down off the high spot, the ground levelled out and revealed an exit from the trees fifty or so metres ahead. Minutes later I was standing on the edge of a broad expanse of deforested land, it was as though I had crossed some invisible line and it took me a few moments to appreciate all the light and open space. This new landscape revived my hope. I was again in the land of people, loggers had been here and chopped down the trees. I surveyed the area and, for as far as I could see, the way through was strewn with stumps, felled trees and loose branches in what was probably the aftermath of an illegal operation. My main concern was getting across it, the way was more obstacle ridden than anything I had yet faced. All my previous movements and techniques, which had by now become second nature, would go out the window. Disheartened, I knew that every yard gained from here on would be a struggle.

Negotiating the larger obstacles like felled trees proved the most difficult and painful, so my method was simply reduced to tumbling over them. By lifting myself up onto one knee, I could reach my arms over the top and push off with the supporting leg. But my outstretched arms often failed to take my weight, causing me to land on my face or fall into a head over heel roll. The wildness of the manoeuvre was torturous for my broken bones. On smaller obstacles, I could reach my arms over to the other side and wheelbarrow forward with my arms, the drawback being that my useless leg would drop from height back onto the ground, leaving me howling in pain. Large tree stumps were easier as I could slide across them on my backside where they were cleanly cut. Some were potentially dangerous, huge slivers of razor-sharp wood spiked up like a row of teeth where the chainsaw cut hadn't been clean, or cut short when the tree was ready to be felled. Falling onto one of these could have easily severed an artery. The space between obstacles was equally problematic and time consuming as there was always a loose branch or an upturned root to climb over or free my clothing from. As soon as I freed myself from one difficulty I encountered another. I fell frequently, smashing my head, cutting my face and tearing my legs and hands. My injured leg was knocked and jerked so frequently that I was more or less in a constant state of pain. It must have been a strange sight, a bloodstained, snow-encrusted man, haphazardly going in and out of sight, tumbling over tree stumps and emerging from the foliage.

I maintained my overwhelming longing to reach the vehicle track before dusk, but the intervening ground stretched out beyond my initial assessment and getting across it was taking up most of the afternoon. I still felt it was achievable and pushed on, stopping only to listen for the reassuring sound of the stream. Following a particularly massive effort I took a rest and emptied the contents of my pockets onto the floor next to me: disposable camera, compass, Brazil shorts, lip balm, mobile phone, coins, a broken lighter, candle, para cord, head torch, Leatherman and cash in a waterproof bag. I couldn't afford to waste even a joule of energy, and my already flagging speed and ability to move was being hampered further as these objects constantly snagged, scraped and dug into my body. I studied the items intently, trying to determine which would be of some further use and which I should discard. I kept the money, the Leatherman and the head torch. I was very sad to lose my Brazil world cup shorts. The decision to leave my disposable camera required some pondering as I couldn't recall if it held the photo of the bear which I had seen days earlier during a trek through the Brasov Mountains.

The immediate area was table-top flat. I pulled a right and broke back into the trees, heading towards the edge of the slope. After some difficult cross graining, I found myself at the edge of a circular-shaped clearing; it seemed like I had been mystically transported to a separate place, far removed from the mountain. There was no breeze and an eerie sort of silence, it was as if the area possessed its own microclimate. For no sound reason I felt disturbed by a strange sense of expectancy, and in the same instant, a shiver ran down my spine. The feeling enveloped me, I remained unmoving and waiting, staring into nowhere, and then, as if inspired by some deep instinct, the urge came to me to make noise and sudden movements. It started to snow, the flakes fell gently around me, coating my head and shoulders, then, out of nowhere, in the space where I was staring stood a large brown bear, only metres away. I couldn't explain why I felt no sense of imminent danger. The bear's presence captivated me like some mythical creature that only I had ever set eyes upon. It was on all fours, motionless, looking straight at me as I stared back in disbelief. I was totally mesmerized; it was the most beautiful thing I had ever seen in my life. Even though

Romania was home to the world's greatest concentration of brown bears, I never dreamed I might actually see one in the wild. It was proof that man had yet to spoil this pristine landscape.

The magical moment lasted only seconds, I broke eye contact and when I looked up the bear had vanished into the trees. I remained suspended in a motionless state, startled and not knowing what to do next, trying to take in what I had just seen. Then reality struck and I realized I faced a real and present danger so I headed back towards the ridgeline. Ten minutes later, I stood at the edge of a firebreak that ran down slope, less than 50 metres below me was the bear making its way down. It must have detected my presence as it stopped momentarily and turned to face me. I slowly dropped one shoulder strap of my Bergen and removed my disposable camera from the top flap. I just made the shot before the bear turned back down the mountain and ran off out of sight, jumping through the deep drifts as it went.

The map and compass no longer served any purpose and the remainder required no thought. There was some excuse to keep each item, practical or sentimental, but I realized my attachment to them might end up killing me. Being rid of my kit made things easier. I was caught up far less often and for a short while I made steady headway. I had completely forgotten about the canoe sack attached to my rear until it caught on a branch some twenty minutes later. I unclipped the remaining buckle and used it to cushion my splintered and bleeding hands. A passage of time followed which I dedicated to beating the clock. It worked for a while mainly due to the generous amount of time I had allocated myself. By the fifth or sixth turn, I had failed twice in succession, so I abandoned the game. Reduced to clambering through with brute force in a series of spurts I entered another blank phase where all I knew was crawling. Thoughts never finished themselves and time was forgotten.

At some later point my awareness returned to the sensation in my feet, which felt grossly swollen and extremely painful. I attempted to ignore it at first, but my ankle seemed to be swelling and my foot started to feel tight against the tongue of the boot. Although the last thing I wanted to do was take my boots off, I started to worry about frostbite and blood clots so stopped to do something about it. I was sure I could successfully massage some sensation back into my feet but instead, I removed my Leatherman tool and used the blade to increase the slit I'd already made at the back of the right heel. After a few moments the tightness went away but the foot still remained dead to all feeling. The left boot proved trickier and more agonizing, I could no longer bend forward enough to reach it, so had to fold my leg beneath me before managing to make an incision. After the pain subsided, I closed the knife, rested for a few seconds and gave a final push to cross the remaining metres of the tree-felled plateau.

It was late afternoon by the time I made it across, and already the sky was in a midway state between light and dark. My route and the stream came back into unison, and once again I was under the canopy of the trees. Snow started to fall, lightly at first before turning heavy. Fat snowflakes spilt through the branches, coating me heavily and obscuring my view. The outer layer of my jacket became sodden, but stayed mercifully dry inside. I came to a stop to catch my breath and carried a mental check on myself: cold and weak. Too cold to stop for long, I continued crawling, dragging myself in small bursts, giving it everything I had for 20 to 30 metres before collapsing into a heap. I told myself it was normal, I had started to feel this way at the end of the previous day and the one before that. I worried about my hands and feet; it felt as though I had stumps at the end of my ankles and wrists. The feeling revived a memory and my mind leaped backwards five years to my time as an army recruit.

In the later stages of Paratrooper training, my eight-man section had been tasked with an overnight OP (Observation Post) during an arduous field-training exercise. We were covertly positioned on a remote hillside with inadequate winter clothing, watching for an enemy played by friendly forces. It was a typically long and cold winter night in the north of England. Within a few hours of first light, every man in the section was going down with the early stages of hypothermia. A member from the Caribbean was highly susceptible to the cold. He started convulsing and going off on bouts of strange and incoherent mumblings; the section machine gunner and I noticed a strange white pus building up around his eyes. We had to hug him to revive some warmth back into his body. Panic stricken, I radioed in for a casevac (casualty evacuation) and salvation arrived in the form of Corporal H, the most brutal staff instructor I encountered throughout my entire military service. He thrashed us with an assortment of exercises up and down the hill in complete darkness, until he felt we were sufficiently warm. Satisfied with his efforts, he departed to the comfort of his sleeping bag while we all fell into shock. At first light, Corporal H was back, rallying us for a full-frontal assault. Rifles in hand, we all crawled out of cover and started to run towards the target. I couldn't feel my feet, they had gone totally dead and felt as though I was running on two stumps. I truly believed I had lost them both to frostbite and they would have to be amputated. Traumatized, I still ran on, desperately trying to keep up with Corporal H in fear of something worse happening.

*

A memory could do so much, this one revitalized my inner strength and nearly raised a smile. I would probably keep my feet after all, and at least now I had a good jacket. I recalled something an instructor said to my platoon on the last day of infantry training, 'You will all be grateful to us one day.'

Another half an hour and my progress was reduced to a chain of clumsy and ill-coordinated movements interspersed with frequent breakdowns of exhaustion. I tried to invite pleasant memories to distract my mind, but by now not even thoughts of my family were enough to revive me or keep me fighting. The idea of dying preyed on my mind a lot, but a counterintuitive voice told me I was being dramatic as nobody ever died of a broken leg. In my delirium, I began to suffer some strange, brief attacks of paranoia, filled with cruel ideas that I deserved everything that had happened to me. Even though I was a not a religious person, I entered into some sort of silent conversation with any god who would listen; a committee of the divine offered me a deal where I would be saved if I agreed to certain terms. I didn't like what they had to offer, but too nervous to say no, I refused to answer and kept crawling, trying to put in some distance as if to escape the barter. A little later I began to ask testing questions of myself: what would I exchange if I could simply survive? Fortune, love, climbing again, not rejoining the military, even a limb? It was as if I was trying to prove something to myself, because in the end I wasn't willing to compromise on any-thing. I was either a cold-hearted bastard or hadn't yet resigned myself to death.

The route had become increasingly undulating over the last fifteen minutes of crawling. I only paid real attention when the area to my right began to rise to impassable heights. Pushed down onto lower ground, I was constrained to follow whatever path the terrain dictated. I couldn't fight a horrible sense of expectation that my way would become blocked again. I tried to dismiss the possibility and pushed on, keeping to my direct route. The way narrowed, and within a hundred metres it disappeared altogether, leaving only the stream and a small impassable cliff. Sad and sickened by the cruelty of it all, I struggled to remove the thought that some malignant entity lurked in the forest and had controlled and planned all this. Scanning the ground further it was clear there was no way up on my side, not any that I had a hope of making. The stream here was wider, deeper and had picked up greater speed. It was more like a small river, about 5 metres wide and looked to be well above head height in depth. I stared sadly into the water, watching the snowflakes land and quickly melt on the surface. I threw a handful of stones at the icicles hang-ing from rocks and plants along the stream's banks; it satisfied me to see them break like glass. The destructive act seemed to revive something in me, my fatalism replaced by aggression, rage and resentment at my continuing bad luck and the seemingly never-ending obstacles put in my way.

My decision to swim across came quickly and with conviction, there could be no room or time for another stuttering performance. I started making sharp purposeful movements, giving myself no margin to delay or bottle out. Hurriedly, I removed my jacket and thermal vest and packed them into my canoe sack. With the bundle packed tightly, I stood up and threw it clear of the water, leaving me with no choice but to go after it. A searing numbness was inflicted on my exposed flesh as I sat at the edge of the bank. The hesitation was long enough for a pile of snowflakes to fill the hollows in my collarbones. I hung my legs over the side and submerged my boots. Trembling like jelly, I dipped down until I was in up to my waist, the good leg taking all my weight. Just as I had braced myself to submerge I remembered my gloves, removed them, tucked one into the other and threw them to the other side. I set my teeth and dropped down quickly until my shoulders went under. The shock expelled all the air from my lungs, the severity delaying any action for a few seconds. Stunned, I paused before kicking off, swimming breast stroke to keep my head dry. I lacked the necessary power and aggression to get across and the current started dragging me downstream. Switching to front crawl, I splashed furiously and within a matter of seconds I had reached the other side.

The impact of the submersion sent me into mild shock, leaving me temporarily incapable of functioning. The cold and exhaustion seemed to catch up with me at once and my situation quickly turned from serious to deadly. I should have rolled in the snow as soon as I was out, but the need for my jacket was too urgent for me to adhere to the disciplined drills I'd learned during my time in the army. Even when I was back in my layers I couldn't revive enough body heat so it was vital I got going again. Seized with a violent fit of shivering I moved off, back into the creeping darkness of the forest, my body shaking in uncontrollable spasms. I hadn't gone far before noticing that my hands were bare, I had forgotten my gloves and was forced to go back for them.

My plan to escape the clutches of the forest and reach the vehicle track had long since been abandoned. I was now moving merely to stay alive. Even though I was convinced that these were my last efforts, I fought against the urge to rest with every instinct I had; some sort of strength I never knew I possessed was forcing me on. It was as though my body and some deeper, hidden and inaccessible part of my mind external to my own will were fighting to stay alive. A sinister eddying mist came down, floating a few feet off the ground and moving in eerie wisps and ghost-like swirls. Dusk faded into black as I dragged my body through these haunting forms and before I knew it darkness had fallen across the forest floor. A deathly silence filled the space between the trees and with it a feeling of immense futility swelled in my heart. I don't know why, but I murmured a call for someone to help me. I had long since stopped being scared, it was just that I didn't want to die on my own, not here on the mountains, and not like this. I pushed on, dragging my way through the trees in what I believed were my final movements. It all felt beyond my control. My head started to feel heavy and my vision started to fade. My body was closing down. Very close to a standstill, I felt the erosion of all hope. I said goodbye to my family. It is an appalling thing to feel all one possesses drain away.

CHAPTER EIGHT

THIRD NIGHT IN THE OPEN

After collapsing, I lay fully stretched out and face down in the snow at the edge of a small open hollow. I allowed my eyelids to drop and this time I didn't make the effort to move. The feeling that I would never get up didn't overwhelm me in the way I'd expected and I found I could consider the idea of my own death without any emotion. If anything, it was a source of solace. I would try to resist it, but my fate now seemed beyond appeal. It was very odd, to believe you are dying, yet somehow feel so detached. That's the good thing about the cold, it freezes everything: you can't feel anything and can't even cry. All I had to do now was keep my eyes closed and I would be at peace – snow, wind, water, rock and trees all effaced from my world. There would be no more broken bones, falls, burning-cold ice and no more sleepless and pain-filled nights.

The cold was starting to take me, entering me stealthily

and working its way through my body like a drug, filling me with a strange bliss. There was a sweet feeling about it which I knew would soon turn me to stone. My consciousness was abandoning the distant regions of my body and I was sliding painlessly away. Gazing up past the slanting peaks of the conifers, a riot of stars filled the sky. I stared at them admiringly, wondering if they would give up something of the mystery of the universe to me if I died. Absorbed and abandoned to the Milky Way, I occupied myself trying to grasp infinity; it seemed a suitable subject for my final hours. A bright star flashed, vanished and reappeared in a different place in the sky. A plane? I pulled out my torch, flashing it on and off, hoping the pilot would see me. I tried to remember the SOS in Morse code but it was a futile attempt. The plane looked high enough to be in outer space and would never see me or understand the intermittent flashings to be a signal for help. A few moments after the aircraft passed from my sight a powerful sense of remorse stirred deep within me. Perhaps the plane was symbolic: a sign of life and hope. Whatever it signified, it brought something in me back to life. With the idea in my head that I might live I mentally prepared myself for the surges of uncontrollable trembling that I would face in my battle to survive another night, though I knew it would take for ever to pass. I withdrew into my jacket and waited. My head was swimming with exhaustion and sleep pulled at my eyelids like a heavy weight, I even had to hold them open with my fingers. The night was an inescapable and frozen prison where I was pitted against the ultimate challenge of staying awake and alive.

CHAPTER NINE

THE LONGEST DAY

Slowly, I initiated my first stiff movements of the day, encouraging my arms back into the jacket sleeves and reaching up to unzip the neck. As my head came through, I felt the sensation of being inside, like waking up in a snow cave. There had been heavy snowfall throughout the night, cocooning my body in a small igloo. I slowly stretched out my legs and cautiously broke a hole through the shelter with my fist. With dawn imminent, I gazed up at the sky waiting for the fading blackness to be diluted pink. I felt no elation when the first rays of light touched the peaks. I sluggishly sat upright, the movement causing snow from the collapsing structure to spill down the back of my neck. I brushed my jacket down and removed my legs from inside the canoe sack. Cold and confused, I stared at my boots and concentrated on the sound of my laboured breathing and the weak and faint beating of my heart. I looked at the pile of snow that had covered me and began cursing this refrigerated hell. Swearing always helped; it was comforting to hear a voice even if it was my own. I swore at my boots, hands and the snow regularly. It made me feel brave to add commentary to my problems, externalizing my emotions to unburden myself and stoking the fire of rage to provide a little warmth. On reflection, the snow shelter had probably saved my life, keeping me a few degrees warmer.

The cold maintained its custom of reminding me I needed to be moving. I felt very calm and clear about what I had to do and it wasn't complicated. Up until now, there had been no true objective or firm plan, only self-preservation. Knowing my very survival rested on my ability to reach refuge by the end of the day somehow took the pressure off. I had to make it, I simply wouldn't last another night and felt a strange reassurance that one way or other it would all be over. Hopefully, someone would find me along the way. I discarded my torn-up canoe sack, and set off following the stream. After less than 50 metres I dropped flat on my face, then several more times in quick succession. I tried to recall if I had had so much trouble when starting off on previous days, it was hard to know as my time on the mountain seemed a blur of uninterrupted crawling and a fit of perpetual shivering. I encouraged myself with the thought that my body needed time to get going properly, then I would regain strength and momentum as soon as my muscles had warmed up. The early part of the day passed without incident and little stress. I was able to put in plenty of small legs of continuous crawling, advancing nearly half a kilometre. I didn't pay much attention to the landscape around me as, like my thoughts, I slid from one place to the next with limited awareness of what happened in-between. Out of nowhere, I remembered an appointment with the real world: my return flight. It was scheduled to depart in a couple of days and if I didn't get back quick, I was going to miss it. I couldn't really afford another ticket, not on my student loan. It was strange to be concerned about something from my normal life; I wondered what I could do about it and began running through a bizarre sequence of events that would allow me to get to Bucharest airport on time.

If I could reach the village by 1700 hours and catch a taxi to Fagaras, I could then hop or crawl onto a train, maybe someone would pick me up and carry me to a seat. A night train to Brasov would only take two hours. Before making a connection, I would need another taxi to the hospital where they would surely give me some crutches. I hoped they didn't bother me by trying to put my leg in a cast as there would be no time for that. I ruminated over my mad plan actually believing I could be at the airport on time. It would save me nearly £300, which would cover most of the cost of a return ticket to Brazil, a trip I had planned for the coming summer. It gave me a renewed sense of purpose to feel as if I still had some connection to my usual life. I kept this foolish and embarrassing idea firmly at the back of my mind, it kept pursuing me for several hours before I realized how absurd and ridiculous it all was.

I quickly re-established a good rhythm, and being free from a lot of the leg pain made all the difference. The cold had started to freeze the joint at my hip and the pain receptors in my body had dulled from repeatedly receiving the same signal and dropped to a lower state of alert. During one of my rest breaks I was hit by an incredible hunger; it had been days since I had last eaten anything substantial. My stomach rumbled in a painful emptiness, initiating a sequence of images of delicious foods in my mind. Although I was ravenous, my hunger was nothing compared to my raging thirst. My mouth and tongue had returned to their rigid, dry state, and although I needed a drink desperately, it meant a 200-metre return journey, a massive distance to go off course. I didn't want to deviate as sooner or later I would hit the stream again, and besides, I had long since discarded my plastic drinking bottle. The ticking clock prevailed over my thirst, so I contented myself with the promise of a fridge full of fizzy and fruit drinks when I made it back. Even though I had no water I decided I should try to eat something, so made an attempt on the battered remains of the sausage rolls which I'd managed to ration. The plastic bag had split so I had lost most of the crumbs, but still I managed to scrape a handful from my trouser pocket even though it was mixed with bits of soil and cotton. Helped down by snow, I succeeded in swallowing what little was left. I dreaded to think what was happening inside me.

I soon found myself back in the rhythm of uninterrupted hand and leg placements. My pattern of movement remained fluid until the path I was confined to petered out among the rocks, turning into a rock-strewn alleyway of stones and boulders with steep cliffs rising to my left. I shook my head in disbelief and began swearing at my never-ending bad luck. The only other passage was to cross the stream and there was no way I would do that again, I would sooner rip my knees open clambering over the rocks. Over the first 20 or so metres I took a few bangs but progress was relatively straight-forward. As I broke further into the alley the going became trickier. The rocks were no more than knee height, but with one after the other I needed a position I could hold, otherwise getting through would take me for ever. After a number of painful experiments I found something that worked. If I elevated my posture to a press-up position, I could reach over the obstruction, one hand at a time, then hop the supporting leg over to the other side. The major difficulty was the injured leg, its hanging weight swung uselessly and pulled at my hip socket. Footing was just as much of a nightmare, occasionally my boot would land on the rounded edge of a stone, causing me to lose balance and come crashing down onto my knee. Going on like this was an exhausting procedure and I hadn't been so out of breath at any time on the mountain. I had covered little over a hundred metres in an hour.

When eventually clear of the stones I reached a ledge with a 10-metre drop down into the stream. This narrow precipice offered the only way through and at less than half a metre wide, it offered just enough space for me to pass. As I cat-walked this rocky outcrop my mind posted images of me falling down into the water and washing up somewhere with the spring melt. From then on I kept tight to the wall and didn't look down. After negotiating my way across I was confronted with more rocks. I resumed my mad hopping movements until they became more cumbersome and had to pull my whole body onto them to slide across. It was slower but a less punishing process than passing over the smaller rocks, the only annoyance being the remaining items in my pockets catching on protrusions in the rocks' surfaces as I slid with my chest pressed firmly against the stone. I finally had enough when the button of my map pocket caught against the sharp edge of a large rock. Attempting to heave myself up, I was pulled down again, landing painfully on my ribs. In a rage I ripped the buttons off my trousers and emptied my pockets of their remaining contents: head torch, money and the Leatherman tool. I noted my strange reluctance to part with my equipment and the strong attachment I felt to these little items that had served me so well, as though I was saying goodbye to a close friend. Apart from the money, which I decided to keep hold of, I was now down to the clothes on my back.

After traversing the larger rocks the ground once again became a clutter of smaller-sized stones with dwindling space in between. I reverted back to my press-up position to get through. The day's early effort had started to tell, with each yard I gained costing an extreme effort. Physically shattered and stupid with the urge to sleep I was becoming comically clumsy and at times my vision faded in and out of focus, causing further disturbance to my coordination. When I looked at any point in the distance, the ground and space vibrated as it does in the haze of a powerful sun. Struggling to contend with my deterioration, my arms buckled under me and my head struck a rock. The blow knocked me for six and left me heavily stunned. I didn't notice the blood pouring down my face until it reached my lips. I mopped the gash with my sleeve, shook my head and blinked in an attempt to regain equilibrium. The dizzy spell lasted a few minutes, a period in which all focus and balance deserted me, as though I was being sucked up into a giant tube. I came to in a state of bewilderment, followed by a sense of urgency. There wasn't much further to go, 20 or so metres. I went to move off but my forehead was still bleeding. I concentrated on stemming the flow of blood by holding a handful of snow against the wound. The coldness made my head ache and my face felt stiff and crispy from three days of dirt and dried blood. I set off again and by the time I reached easier ground I was wrecked. The gruelling toil of crawling off the slopes had severely taxed my endurance, but rock alley was massacring me.

My hands were frozen to the bone from contact with the snow and the coldness of the rocks. I clenched them into tight fists and withdrew them into my sleeves, waiting a while until they had warmed a little. I wanted to rest for longer but I had already lost too much valuable time covering such a short distance. I rolled back onto my belt buckle and resumed crawling, this time on my forearms and elbows. After twenty minutes and a couple of hundred metres, the stream was back within sight. I found a spot where the banks weren't high and wriggled over to the edge. With a firm grip of a tree root, I dropped my other hand into the water and quickly brought a few drops to my lips. Even though my desire to drink was insatiable, I allowed myself no more than ten minutes drinking time before moving off again. There was always that voice in my head, telling me that it was a race against time and that I should get moving. I followed the stream for some distance before veering off into a long gentle ascent. The trees opened up, leaving me exposed to the wind on a narrow section of the slope, and in the far distance I saw plumes of black smoke rising up into the sky. I wondered where it could be coming from before I remembered the huge factory on the outskirts of Fagaras. Four days earlier I'd been unimpressed, thinking it a scar on such a beautiful landscape, now I couldn't be more pleased to see it. Irrationally, the sight of the smoke made me want to shout out for help even though its source was many miles away, but my weak calls were snatched and taken away by the wind. I felt so near, yet knew I still had a long way to go.

Elevating myself back up to my three-legged crawl I shuffled my way excitedly up slope, shoulders hunched to protect me from the prevailing wind that picked up as I neared the brow. Coming over the top, a prolonged and icy blast of shrieking wind flew into me from the side, pricking my ears and making the fabric of my clothing flap like torn sails. My woollen hat was snatched from my head and blown down slope, snow dust, stinging ice fragments and forest debris blew into my eyes and my hair twisted in all directions. Wanting to retrieve my hat before it was carried further away, I flipped over onto my backside and dropped down out of the whip of the wind, propelling myself down the other side as fast as I was able without harm to my leg. At the bottom of the slope the stream snaked back into my path and I was enveloped by forest once more. Aware that the slopes were steepening and closing in at the flanks, I continued to follow the natural contour of the valley to keep me on course. As my already constricted passage became more hostile and confined, I began to feel like a small creature, imagining how vast everything must appear to the forest fauna. I tried to think of an animal that moved at a comparable speed to me and finally settled on a hedgehog: conjuring up such rubbish kept me occupied, helping me not to notice the pain or cold with such intensity. Fostering images of hedgehogs, bears and other forest animals, I let them play theatre in my mind. Soon after, I thought about the delicious pink, iced cakes cooked by my mother, Count Dracula in his Transylvanian castle and a disastrous game for the blind I had made for a school design project.

It had started snowing again, adding an extra layer of quietness to my surroundings as though the entire area had been soundproofed. The flakes were dropping diagonally, and as the wind picked up through the pines, they changed pattern, sparse at first, and circling as they fell. As the cold wind came driving down off the slopes, the snow came whirling in thick and fast. I stared up at the dense ceiling of white, heavy clouds that loomed high above. Although I was certain the blizzard could wipe me out, there was something of an excitement to the conditions, like that of a hurricane or fantastic electrical storm. I was amidst the haze and flurry of a whirlwind of snowfall, yet felt a subtle nervous energy triggered by my struggle with nature. It was dark matter, there was something in me that relished the challenge. As I fought my way through the weather, I crossed paths with a small wildcat which I believed to be a lynx. It was a sighting even more miraculous than my encounter with the bear. I froze and stared in awe as it continued moving in my direction. The cat had sharp, pointed ears and its coat was touched with a thin mat of snow, but the fur on its side was a golden brown with black flecks and white on its belly. Its movements lacked the stealth to indicate that it might be out hunting, more likely it was caught in the blizzard on its way to shelter, just as I was. I was sure it noticed me as it moved on but it showed no signs of fear or aggression; the storm was our common foe.

After four hours of crawling, disaster struck again – my route along the low ground formed into a small bottleneck. Steep-sided grey rocky outcrops, impassable barriers to me, blocked my path on either side of the stream which ran in a gully straight down the middle. I was not capable of dragging my body uphill to find another way out, nor could I go back either, having already taken the only possible route out. I sat looking into the water, shaken into disbelief, knowing I would have to get into it again. I could see 30 metres downstream before it curved off out of sight. The water ran shallow and peacefully enough to convince me the task was doable. I decided my best bet was to lean against the sides of the ravine and employ whatever movements I could improvise. This time I would have to keep my jacket and vest on or I would never see them again.

Without further hesitation I got straight into the water, which didn't even come up to my knees. A couple of conveniently placed rocks assisted my passage to the far side, which looked to offer me the best support. With one hand always fixed against the wall I began making my way downstream, all action going through my supporting good leg. The method was peculiar, but tried and tested. I would make small twisting movements, pivoting from toes to heel and vice versa. Each manoeuvre gained no more than a boot's length, but with a part of my foot firmly planted, I was always stable. Where possible I would insert my fingers and hands into holds and cracks in the wall, facilitating movement with more confidence and security. If there was sufficient leverage, I could hang from the rock face, lift my good leg and swing a good 10 inches forward. I just had to be careful not to make a splash and watch for the thin skin of treacherous ice that covered most of the wall.

As I made headway downstream my progress slowed and demanded more attention. The stream bed was littered with rocks that were too big and awkward to hop onto or over. I had a near miss hopping up onto one, my ill-coordinated footing caused it to roll, which sent me crashing forward into the water, smashing my knee against it. I managed to remain upright, but my injured leg had folded and was being crushed beneath my weight. Wailing in pain, I clawed at the wall trying to lift myself to a standing position. Though I was tempted to put my hands down, I was determined to keep my gloves and sleeves dry. The crash had drenched my trousers and given my jacket a good splash, but it was still dry inside. I was lucky to have been in shallow waters, if I had fallen further forward it would have been game over.

Fortunately the water was for the most part crystal clear, allowing me to see the stream bed, and knowing what was coming made it easier to direct my feet and channel my concentration into being extra cautious in exactly the right places. After passing the awkward-sized rocks, I waded into deeper water. I rolled the bottom of my jacket up and tugged the draw cord tight, exposing my stomach. The next difficulty was large, flagstone-like rocks just beneath the surface, some as wide as the length of my body. Improvising a new technique to overcome them slowed my progress down to less than 30 metres in half an hour. Carefully, I would lower my knee down onto the rock's surface, leaving me submerged up to my waist. I used an adaptation of my toe to heel technique, instead pivoting on my knee so that my back faced my intended direction. From this position, I could plant my foot and use the wall to lift to standing. It was a queer technique, but the only kind of forward progress I could produce.

After an hour in the stream the coldness of the water began to take its effect. The shock of the last time I'd swum had stolen a great amount of body heat, but the exposure now was a prolonged agony. My hands and lower body felt dead and heavy with cold. My feet felt nothing of the hard surface below, the only receptors were the muscles in my thigh aching at bearing my weight. As the bend straightened out I could see that the way ahead promised more of the same, steep-sided walls of rock offering no way out. I imagined standing for hours, freezing horrendously until my leg gave way, eventually washing up somewhere a frozen corpse. The idea of a retreat came to mind, but I had in effect passed the point of no return. I swore bitterly and prepared for another push. Concentrating on my balance and foot placements, I followed the sides for another half hour, struggling on like an ant wading through treacle.

The stream gradually opened up into a bowl shape, the sides grew taller and were smoothed out from thousands of years of cascading spring melt. Running straight down the middle of the channel a series of rocks rose from the water, forming stepping stones to the far end. I figured I could bridge the gap by cross grading, cutting valuable metres and saving precious time over contouring the sides. I stared out into the bowl, sussing out my chances of making it across. The water level was my main concern; it was already up to my navel and rising. Getting from stone to stone wouldn't be easy.

Standing upstream from the first rock I let the current push my legs against its sides. I took this chance for a brief rest and lay my chest flat on the surface, closing my eyes and thinking of home. I made sure the jacket draw cord was pulled tight and rolled it up another couple of inches before making my move towards the next rock a couple of metres away. The current nearly took my leg as I stepped out into the stream's flow. So from then on I maintained an especially firm grip on the rock's angular edges as I worked my way downstream. Having reached the limit of my support, and too cold and impatient to pivot from toe to heel, I decided to risk a hop. With one hand still fixed to the rock behind me, I made a jump forward sideways on: one more of those and I'd be there. I lunged with an outstretched arm for protection and grasped the rock, took another rest before repeating the sequence, and moved from stone to stone until I had neared the end.

By this time I'd been in the water for nearly two hours and it was without doubt the coldest I had ever been, I was shivering so frantically I couldn't even swear. Edging my way to the downstream side of the penultimate rock, I discovered there was no way across to the narrow channel ahead; the final rock was too far out of reach – as much as 5 metres away. My body started to convulse, I wasn't sure if it was shivering or if I was trying to cry. It seemed that behind every little victory or overcoming of an obstacle lay only a gateway to more suffering. I kept falling into the trap of thinking I had made it to safety and with each disappointment my mental state descended further towards breaking point.

I calmed down and tried to plan a way out. My best chance was to return the way I had come then follow the sides back up. I was deterred by the fact that it had taken nearly an hour just to cross the bowl and reach my current position, and realistically it would be the same time again for a retreat. I knew that moving up the sides would be even slower. The whole idea was unthinkable and unbearable. My alternative was to risk hopping my way across to the flanks or the next rock, but the distance was too great to attempt such a manoeuvre. With the water level already up to my navel, I had no chance. I knew I would fall in. I rested my body onto the stone, tortured over what to do next. I had been well and truly broken, but wouldn't even be rewarded with the indignity of being able to give up. I was trapped and freezing to death.

I stared out toward the end of the bowl wondering what lay beyond it; if I could be certain of a way out I would swim. I tried to accustom myself to the idea, screwing up my courage to put it into execution. Suddenly enraged, I shouted out in a burst of aggression, as if to startle myself out of the mire of self-pity into which I'd sunk. Then I began swearing even more. After a mouthful of obscenities I climbed up onto the rock, quickly removed my clothing and set to work, tucking the sleeves into the body of the jacket and screwing the bundle into a tight ball before tying it off with the remaining length of para cord. Naked from the waist up, I lowered myself down off the rock into the water, carefully sinking until my shoulders went under. With the clothes bundle held above my head, I kicked off against the side of the rock and began a one-armed swim. Both legs sank straight away and began scraping along the bottom. Gasping for breath, I pushed off from the stream bed and paddled frantically. It was hardly swimming and I could barely hold a straight line, but within seconds I had made it across without getting my bundle wet. It had felt like I'd been in the water for ever.

Immediately I placed my dry clothes safely onto the top of the rock and pulled myself up so that only my legs were in the water. In a series of fast but ill-coordinated movements I plucked at the knot holding my clothes together and put my vest and jacket back on. For a few moments I just sat there, trying to take in what had just happened. The army river crossings in Scottish winter time had been a piece of cake in comparison. I shook my head at the absurdity of it all: a man with broken bones swimming down a freezing mountain stream in the Transylvanian Alps. It felt like a crazy bad dream and was every bit as ridiculous as my thoughts told me, but the gravity of the situation had justified the risks. My minor success made me realize that I could have eliminated unnecessary suffering and saved plenty of time by swimming from the start. It would have only been a few minutes to cover the same distance, instead of the two hours it had taken me on one shaky leg. But to swim on blindly from my current position was to invite disaster. I knew nothing of what lay ahead or for how long I would be in the water. It was always in my mind that if I got my jacket wet, I was as good as dead.

Beyond the bowl, the gulley narrowed into a small cave of 20-metre high sheer rock walls that almost met overhead. I couldn't tell how deep it went, but I could see light spilling in from the other end. Inside it felt eerily silent, except for the drip of water sounding out a dull, doom-like note as it fell from the ceiling into the stream. There was almost a peacefulness about it; it was a refuge from the whipping wind and driving snow. Channels carved out beneath the rock walls caused the flow to become gentler and the water level to drop below my knees. The stream flowed silently and only a few gentle flakes of snow slipped down through the gaps above. Making my way downstream was now less troublesome, the stream bed was flat and uninterrupted by rocks and sudden drops, so I no longer feared falling or required the same intense concentration as I did before. I hoped this change signalled a way out, but on moving deeper inside, the sound of my slight movements caused a deathly echo around the chamber. A sense of abandonment hit me and all I could think about was leaving the water. Home was a more distant thought.

As I neared the light coming through the exit I began to triumphantly anticipate being back on dry land. I stepped back out into the open and scouted the ground to my front, but there was no sight of a way out, just another stretch of water enclosed by high rock walls. Distraught at the discovery, I came to rest and made a fist to crack the ice that had formed on my cold and sodden gloves. To cover only a hundred metres I had been in the water for just under three hours and my body was showing clear signs of hypothermia. My condition degenerated as I passed through an exposed section where the wind angled in a mixture of snow and rain almost horizontally, coming at me like a razor and hitting me in the face and eyes. The icy gusts obliterated the shape of the snow mounds on the stream's high rocky banks as a frosty vapour of cold air rose off the water's surface into my jacket like a liquid which seemed to penetrate me to the marrow.

'God help me.'

I remained fixed to the left bank, shuffling from heel to toe, having to rest more and more frequently. I covered a long stretch without caring to look ahead, taking each new bend without expectation, until finally I saw a break on the other side. Twenty metres downstream the tree line opened up and staggered to an end, presenting a small slope with reed patches coming up through the snow. The last obstacle was to cross to the other side, I would have to swim. With one arm holding my clothes aloft and the other in the water, I pushed off. Sensing my own desperation I told myself not to get complacent. Closing in, I lunged for the side and threw my clothes bundle up onto dry land. The lower edge of the bank was a metre above water level, beyond that the ground sloped upwards. Taking a firm grip of the reeds I tried to lift myself out of the stream, but it wasn't until my third attempt that I was able to anchor my good leg up. Water flushed heavily down my trousers and splashed back down into the stream as I worked the rest of my body up. Collapsing into a heap, I lay face down on the ground, in spite of my precarious position at the foot of the bank. It was only the tickle of fresh snow falling on my naked back that reminded me I had forgotten to put my jacket on. With a vague feeling of relief I towelled myself dry with the inside of my jacket and put my base layer back on. I was still shaking, but only in part from the cold, I realized my nerves were shot to pieces.

'Get going,' I commanded myself.

Keeping a tight grip on the reeds I began worming my way up, digging the toe end of my boot into the ground and pushing off, inching forward as the bank steepened. It was slow progress as one slip and I'd have been sent tumbling back down into the stream. My water-logged boots were heavy and squelched and gurgled with every push. My feet were so devoid of sensation that I couldn't feel the heel of my right boot working its way off each time I dug it into the ground and pressed through it. I continued to force a way up until it was too late, the boot had become very loose and was off my foot before I could react. I turned and watched it bounce down the slope as if in slow motion. It fell into the water, landing with a splash. After going under for a fraction of a second, the boot resurfaced and was quickly taken down stream, bobbing on the surface before disappearing from sight.

'Now I'm fucked!'

I would probably lose my foot within hours.

I fell to the ground and cradled my head in my hands. I tried to cry but couldn't, I didn't have anything in me other than a few short, pitiful and muffled convulsions of breath and weak chest heaves. I could no longer understand anything that was happening to me and was attacked by a multitude of confused and angry thoughts that swarmed in a psychedelic haze inside my brain, caught in some halfway state between consciousness and destruction. The acrid sting of bile in my mouth caused me to retch and I almost blacked out. In that moment I wanted the earth to open up and swallow me. I don't remember now how long I lay there with no desire to move, perfectly still and beyond caring, expecting the cold would soon win its battle with me. Traumatized, my body was no longer able to identify pain; in fact it had simply gone beyond every pain boundary I thought I had. It wasn't that I was beaten, I just couldn't move any further. I considered that if it was ever discovered how far I'd come, nobody could say I'd quit. I had tried so hard, there was just nothing more to give.

The rest of my memories went down in a sort of blur of faded pictures. Then I ceased thinking and listened to the sound of my breathing and my heart hammering audibly in my chest. It felt like I'd been there an eternity. As if by some instinctive survival measure I moved my head up and down and side to side, as if acknowledging something I didn't yet understand; I wasn't really sure why, but maybe my body was trying to tell me I was still alive. Small movements became larger and then I sat up. I couldn't stop looking at myself and began touching my hands and legs, massively impressed by my capability to bend my fingers at three joints. Then I started to understand. I had sat there waiting and expecting the worst, my mind and body totally out of sync, one finished and the other waiting for the order to move. It was as though the positive channel in my brain had cobwebbed over and forgotten the strong-willed sentiments that had kept me going up until this point. Still, after all that had happened, my body was willing to keep going, it was my mind that showed weakness, got upset and threw little tantrums. All I had to do was to endure; to stop now would be unforgivable.

I regained some control over the chaos in my mind, realizing it really was all in my head, just like the bastard instructors at the training depot had told us. I remembered a young suicide, a Paratrooper Corporal from the 2nd Battalion, just as I had completed recruit training. He had jumped off the top of a multi-storey car park over a problem with some girl. I had no notion of the temptation to which he had succumbed, but I did know that I was just as responsible for my actions as he was. If I didn't move, it would be as if I was jumping off that car park too. I came to the firm conclusion that I would actually be committing suicide if I didn't try to keep going. Not telling my body to move was a deliberate act, it would be killing myself only because I could no longer handle the difficulty of my situation and not because my body couldn't move. The reasons, motives and circumstances mattered not: I was capable of moving, therefore I had to issue my body the command. A hot, wet tear ran down my cheek. I lifted my chest from the ground and started crawling. To save myself was to move, then move again, it was the same first movement repeated. It never ceased to amaze me how much suffering my body could endure.

As I dragged myself I began to think with an alarming clarity that hadn't been with me since the fall. The distances and terrain I had had to cover in my condition were staggering, almost imponderable, yet I had come actively seeking a challenge and hoped that some excitement or meaningful event would come my way. Now I was stranded in this lonely place and involuntarily pitted against something harder than anything I had sought or believed I was capable of overcoming. Looking at my surroundings, I began to understand and accept my lot, no matter how brutal it was revealing itself to be. The horror of death no longer affected me and for the first time I removed all ideas and hopes of a rescue from my mind – they were useless, only serving to weaken my resilience and crush my spirit. My determination and resolve to keep moving could only be undermined by pinning my faith and life on someone else. Knowing this gave me the chance to confront my struggle independently, whatever my ultimate fate there was some excitement in understanding that it was all down to me.

As I pressed on, the terrain and scenery remained constant, it felt as though I had been dragging myself through the same spot for hours. I was still inside the clutches of the forest with no sign of the vehicle track. The wind in the high trees blew and the boughs made sinister creaking sounds. Where the snowfall was sparse, the forest floor offered a soft bed of pine needles. Although they felt soft and warm beneath me, my hands were too numb to notice them splintering into my palms. I came to my first stop in half an hour when my arms eventually gave way and I dropped into a heap. Looking up through the trees and out to the sky, enjoying my few moments of rest, it was tempting to stop for longer, but I knew I couldn't. My raging thirst had returned with a vengeance and my mouth was back to its desiccated state. I had been in the water for three hours, yet not felt the slightest compulsion to drink from it. It had seemed wrong to poison myself with the substance that was slowly killing me. I moistened the inside of my mouth with the fresh snow from the ground and decided I could reach the track within half an hour. I tried to play beat the clock, but after a few attempts, even plentiful time limits defeated me. Each time I looked up, my destination seemed to be getting no closer. I forced my mind to channel itself into all the good things worth living for, encouraging happy memories as well as enticing possibilities for the future. I also made dramatic promises to myself: as long as there was still a single breath of air in my body I would never give up. For all the many emotions that friends, family and good times could inspire, my true motivation was dominated by countless thoughts and images of food. These *Braveheart* moments were always short lived. Now I was reduced to the status of a stray animal, wanting nothing more than food, water and somewhere warm to rest. My desire for food grew so strong it temporarily eclipsed my very instincts for survival. Images of plump roast chickens, lemon meringue pies and sparkling water ran through my mind, leaving little room for other thoughts.

I'd now been crawling away from the snow long enough for my body to start warming up noticeably. The first sign was a peculiar new sensation in my hands; they felt extraordinarily thin and ached at the fingers. It was as though I had skeleton hands, and if I were to remove my gloves I would see nothing but bones with all the flesh and tissue frozen and stripped away. As my core started to warm, the pain in my leg went up a notch. It wasn't as bad as it had been, but the cold had undoubtedly frozen away a generous share of the agony, especially over the last twenty-four hours. I started to look at my body as an amazing survival machine, if it was too cold it would draw all the blood away from the extremities and into its core, anything to stay alive, even at the cost of lost fingers, toes or limbs.

My attention soon returned to food. I couldn't be sure what came first, the thought or the mirage-like sighting of a cake in front of me. At first, I looked away and shook my head as if to encourage some sense to return, but the cake was still there: a huge, pink, iced Victoria sandwich like my mother used to bake. Ignoring it I moved on, but after 50 metres it was back again, sitting just out of my reach. I had seen the same cake years before during a long hard battle march in the army. By the third sighting I was tempted to divert from my path to get my hands on it. I stopped briefly to watch it before continuing along my route. The hallucinations came and went in a constant slide show as I moved between the trees. An array of shapes and images passed before my eyes, some were still and took on cartoonish appearances, others followed along beside me, becoming animated. They looked solid enough to touch and my eyes told me that they were real. A rolling theatre of sharp secondary colours performed on the forest floor against the backdrop of trees. Out of nowhere, memories of *Willo the Wisp,* a children's cartoon, jumped into my mind. I remembered my brother and me hiding behind the sofa each time the wicked character Evil Edna appeared. A ringing sound in my ears slowly turned into the theme tune followed by the unmistakable voice of the narrator, Kenneth Williams. It wouldn't go away, amusing me at first, before becoming an annoyance. Soon after I started to see shapes and faces of people I knew, and the harder I stared, the more they came to life. Some looked demonic and spooky, their mouths contorting into strange shapes and vivid colours. Then out of nowhere, Evil Edna, a walking cartoon TV set with a witch's face on the screen stepped out from behind a tree and pointed her antennas in my direction, threatening to zap me with an electrical shock. I put my head down and moved on, leaving Edna behind. I stared at my route intently, focusing my attention and trying to ignore my illusions.

From then on I decided to crawl with my head down, fixing my eyes on the ground immediately in front of me. The plan worked for a while, although without the distraction I felt more pain and noticed the cold. Unexpectedly, something else grabbed my attention, a large expanse of light giving a splendid backdrop to the tall pine trees. I knew what it could mean, but tried to keep it a secret from myself to save disappointment. With less than 50 metres to go I hurried forward as fast as I could.

'One more push!'

Head fixed down, I crawled urgently, trying to suppress something inside me resembling excitement and hope. Within minutes I broke free of the forest and out onto the vehicle track. The immediate sense of security was overwhelming. I remained stunned, silent and motionless, all at once emptied of the emotions I had carried off the mountain and through the forest. Despair and fear evaporated, releasing their grip on me as I left the trees. The vehicle track was my salvation, a man-made sign of life that marked my gateway back into the world. I knew for certain where I was, I had walked up this very path only days before. Taking a prolonged rest I began to reflect on my ordeal, it felt I was reviewing four years of my life, not four days. Even though I was still far from safety, all I wanted was to shut my eyes, sleep and relax. I must have dozed off a few times but automatically woke in a state of panic, checking to see if the track was still there. It took some time to get myself together, but in spite of my terrible condition the jubilation of being so close to escape eclipsed all my other concerns.

CHAPTER TEN

OUT FROM THE WILD

The first stretch of track was flat for a couple of hundred metres. Adopting the table posture that had served me so well before, I began shuffling forward, bringing my good knee up to my hands in a movement that was now second nature. Having no right boot made pushing off uncomfortable, and I kept scraping the top of my foot harshly along the gravel, which only had a thin covering of snow to protect my skin against the sharp stones. I thought about trying to force the left boot onto my right foot, but knew it would take too long and be too much trouble; I just wanted to keep moving while I could. After twenty minutes or so the ground started to decline, allowing me to slide along on my ass. By the time I had reached the bottom it had stopped snowing and the sky cleared; it was the first break in the weather for hours. Abruptly I came to a stop, feeling compelled to look back. Stretched high above the forest, I could see the range of snow-covered mountaintops stained pink by the setting sun. They stood there in all their majesty, still and untouched, indifferent to human endeavour and what they had done to me.

Some distance down the track was a small village, I tried to figure out how much further I had to go, guessing at between 3 kilometres or as many miles. I checked my watch, it was three thirty, which meant I had just over an hour of daylight left. Early attempts at crawling again were difficult, I made a few purposeful bursts but they were more like false starts. It was taking longer than normal to build up some body heat and establish a rhythm again and even when I did, I couldn't stop thinking about my bootless foot, worrying that my toes would go black long before I reached help.

I had started to hallucinate again, but this time I was able to ignore the unusual images that came before me. Occasionally, I would turn back to take a look at the mountains. Fascinating and frightening, they reminded me of why I was here and what I had to do. Each time I looked back, none of what had happened seemed real, the events of the last four days felt so distant and alien. My dreamlike state evaporated as I noticed the looming darkness creeping up on me, realizing that I had to use whatever daylight remained in order to cover as much ground as possible. As the dragging continued I would stop every so often and call out for help, but my cries were weak and faint as I could barely manage to expel enough air to make my voice carry. I had slowed dramatically again and was hardly able to carry out more than three consecutive heaves at a time. Over the course of the next kilometre, the weakening began to feel progressively more intense; for all my determination I knew I couldn't prolong the struggle indefinitely. When I could no longer hold my focus, my mind took me off on more of its random and uncontrollable journeys, filling my head with bizarre images, pointless fantasies and cryptic philosophies. I envisioned a kaleidoscope of comforting and illusory scenes and my part in them unfolding in a drunken, dreamlike way. I would come back to my senses occasionally, only to be sucked back in to the whirlpool of lost and valueless thoughts. As long as I kept moving nothing else mattered. I had dragged myself on every level of emotion and had exhausted them all. Self-preservation was all I cared for, yet it was no longer me that wanted it; some innate human instinct, the pure essence of survival was battling to hang on to life. Strength of mind and physical fitness no longer counted, now something deeper and darker conducted my movements. For long stretches I recalled little other than the infrequent blissful moments of rest.

I had been following the track for well over an hour when it occurred to me that I should try to stand. Hardly noticing my injured leg any more, and hoping that the joint had fused or frozen enough to hold my weight, I believed I might be able to walk. The possibilities of what I was about to attempt initiated a small wave of enthusiastic energy in me and with it this newborn hope banished my earlier fears and regrets. I dragged myself eagerly towards the trees at the right-hand edge of the track. Gripping tightly onto an overhead tree branch, I slowly lifted myself up, my good leg taking all the weight. With one hand still clasped around the branch I began to experiment with my injured leg, placing the sole of my foot to rest flat on the ground and allowing it to get used to the sensation of light pressure, which sent out mild vibrations that ran from my foot to hip. Gradually, I transferred a small portion of weight across before quickly relieving it. I was losing invaluable light, but if I could somehow manage to walk, I would make the time back up and bring it all to an end that much sooner. I considered hopping, but quickly forgot the idea and carried on testing the basic functionality of my leg. Becoming bolder in small stages, I eventually allowed something close to a half share of weight onto the foot of my bad leg. For a fraction of a second it remained bearable before it gave way. I heard the familiar scrape of bone followed up by a sharp snap that felt like a new break. Stabbed by pain, the leg gave way and left me a crumpled heap on the verge.

It was a few minutes before I could summon the strength to stand up again. I knew I had to try to walk; the way things were progressing I would be crawling until frozen into a block of ice. Swaying on one leg, I let the left foot rest gently on the snow. I tried again, this time with the bent-knee and tiptoes technique that had worked so well crossing the streams. The pain level was bearable and my balance precarious, and for a few seconds my injured leg could hold around a third of my weight. I managed a few small steps before stumbling forward, ending up on the ground again. I lay winded but undeterred, knowing that I would be able to walk if I could find a stick to use as a crutch. Feeling a surge of purpose and confidence, I dragged myself back onto the track and began to scour the verge looking for a walking aid. After only a couple of minutes I came to an unscheduled stop, distracted by the unusual sounds coming from my guts. There were strange convulsions originating from the pit of my stomach, initially a subtle creeping ache, followed by a huge contraction that felt as though my stomach was being ripped apart. I writhed in agony, screaming as though I were being tortured in the worst possible way. For fifteen to twenty seconds the pain remained absolutely constant and merciless. I wondered what the hell was happening to me, a shattered leg was nothing compared to this. It was by far the most terrible pain I had ever suffered in my life. I lay still in the foetal position, panting heavily and in utter dread that the pain would return. I realized I had wet and messed myself. Moments later, I suffered a second attack, this time it settled after a few short and mild convulsions. I waited anxiously, trying to fathom the causes. Whatever the reason, I was in serious trouble and this was a clear warning that time was running out.

There were fewer than thirty minutes of daylight remaining. Apprehensive of any signs that the convulsions would return, I dragged myself on, still searching for a stick to use as a crutch. The path began to meander in slow lazy bends as it dropped away from the high ground, and the forest gradually closed in on the track's edges. I passed through a section where the verges were scattered with deadfall, rocks, rusty coils of barbed wire and discarded pieces of metal from old fencing. I eagerly assessed the assortment for a walking stick, and was especially excited by the barbed wire, liking the noise it made as it uncoiled like a spring at my disturbance. Most of the dead branches were either too short or too thin and brittle. I thought what great firewood it would make, and how getting through the nights wouldn't have been half as bad if my lighter hadn't broken. Not finding anything, I considered binding two short sticks together with the remaining length of para cord I still had in my breast pocket, but decided it was a rubbish idea. I continued my rummaging further along, eventually coming across a sizeable branch. It was a good few feet too long and had several smaller branches coming off it so I set to work stripping away the off shoots. The biggest problem was its length; I would have to snap it. Despite my efforts, the wood was stronger and more flexible than I had imagined, the saw from my Leatherman would have been useful and I cursed myself for having discarded it. In the end I stood on top of it and wrenched the other end up until it snapped. I almost fell and only kept my balance with the help of a nearby fence post. It was an untidy break, but it would have to do.

Holding my position and taking up all my weight on the working leg, I cautiously swung the broken one forward together with the stick. Distributing my weight between the two, I quickly brought my good leg level in a mad hop. And that was it; I could walk! Feeling a surge of jubilation I shuffled my way back onto the track and tried again, marvelling at my new-found ability; it almost felt like a superhero power. After a succession of competent steps, I decided to turn the stick upside down. The remains of a broken branch at the other end came out at an angle, forming a V-shape, which I thought might serve as a crude shoulder crutch. The intention was to transfer all my weight through the stick, saving unnecessary trauma to my injured leg as well as allowing me to move quicker. I attempted a few small steps to see if the adaptation was workable, but I quickly found out the hard way that this was no good when the jacket material under my arm caught on the stick's crook, trapping my arm and sending me tumbling sideways. I landed heavily, cracking the side of my head on the ground, but quickly got back on my feet and continued my slow walk, this time reverting back to the original technique.

I fell every few steps but the duration between each fall grew. With practice my technique became more useful and I was able to cover ground with satisfying ease. Although I took no independent steps with my injured leg, with support from the stick it could bear my weight long enough for me to make a small pace forward with my good leg. I found I could move far quicker by making small shuffling bursts instead of big ones, covering between 10 and 15 metres in fewer than thirty seconds. As I became more adept I began to experiment; the significant variation was to bring my good leg forward first, then to draw the staff and my bad leg level. I alternated between the two, changing after each brief stop. When I mastered both, I gained confidence, repeating the movements with faith. Before long, I was walking fluidly and with such ease that I was able to step ahead of the planted foot.

As the way ahead opened up, the path straightened and descended some more until it eventually disappeared into the trees in the distance. Snow-covered fields separated the woods and the track, and to my right was a steep grey cliff. I had been walking for an hour when I reached a recognizable feature, a narrow arch-shaped tunnel carved into the side of the rock face. Seeing it had an extraordinary effect on my morale. It was the place I had crawled inside with my head-lamp days before.

Darkness was descending as the track led me back into the woods. I turned one final time to take a look at the mountains and stayed watching them, remaining fixed until they faded into dark, sinister outlines. The realms of suffering that had existed up there for me seemed almost unimaginable now. I turned my back on them for the last time and followed the track into the shadows of the trees. Overhead the branches on either side stretched out across the sky forming a roof over the track, giving the impression of walking through a long archway. In a quick transition the wind and tempera-ture dropped and I became enveloped in darkness and si-lence. There was an eerie yet comforting familiarity about being back in the woods; the stillness was punctuated only by the sound of my breathing and the echo of my footsteps crunching through crisp layers of frozen snow. The curtain of branches overhead occasionally revealed a clear night sky, the stars were out, shining brilliantly and lighting my way, just as they had lit up so many of my darkest nights in the army and making me forget my keenest sorrows. I greeted my distant friends; it was another night under their reassur-ing light. There was a tranquillity and peacefulness in the air, the splendour and solitude blotted out all bitterness and re-sentment and for a short time I felt untroubled and verged on something resembling happiness. With restored equanimity, I began to understand that once a man gets truly caught up in an event, he no longer has any fear of it.

After leaving the forest I covered over 1,500 metres without incident, it was the longest I had gone without falling. Although it was solid progress the calf muscle on my good leg cramped often and my left arm was killing me from bearing my weight through the stick. Every couple of hundred metres or so, I would gently lower myself down onto the soft mounds of snow formed on the verge and take five minutes rest. Catching my breath, I took great pleasure in massaging my calf and restoring some heat back into my freezing hands by cupping them together and urinating into them before sticking them both between my legs. Although numb they didn't yet have frostbite, but each movement of my fingers opened and closed deep crevices that oozed with liquid and blood. I hoped the urine would cauterize them. Following each break I continued to make good progress and kept it up for the next 3 kilometres and, with growing confidence, I put my right hand inside my jacket pocket and kept it there. The hand took twenty minutes to return to normal and was the warmest any part of my body had been in four days. I no longer noticed my exposed foot as there was no pain or burn from the cold. Without looking, I wouldn't have been able to tell one foot had a boot and the other not. It wasn't a good sign.

It was nearing the fourth hour since I'd reached the track and the second hour since I'd been able to walk. The amount of ground I'd covered made me understand that the stick was the narrow margin upon which my survival rested. I would never have made it this far if I hadn't managed to get up onto my feet. My path through the woods intermittently gave away height in steep sections, meandering downwards in sharp horseshoe turns. I descended slowly, making careful placements with my walking stick and upon reaching level ground, the track widened and its surface smoothed out. Although the distance I had covered along the track already seemed greater than remembered, it still felt as though I was leaving the wilderness behind and breaking away from an adversary.

Bright orange lights from the town of Fagaras flickered with a cheerful brilliance in the far-off distance. I looked on yearningly, imagining what the townspeople were doing in the comfort of their own homes, watching football, eating warm stew by the fire, making love, drinking beer, all oblivious to my hell in their own backyard. I pictured my family eating dinner in front of the TV and my friends out drinking in Owens Park student village bar, or some camp NAAFI or pub in a garrison town. It seemed surreal that everyone was getting on with life while I was out here. I checked the time. I hadn't realized it was so late – the hours drifted by unnoticed after dark. The lights disappeared as I followed the track behind more trees, but when I came out the other side I could still make out a faint glow of orange hovering in the sky. I made my way uphill through another long section of trees. The track cut through in a neat straight line and when I reached the top I could see the lights again, many miles away. My course dropped down slightly, leading me to a fork in the road. I came to a standstill and tried to figure out which one to take. I was sure that the right-hand track lead to Fagaras and a small village was within a mile or two of the fork.

'And the left road?'

The taxi driver had taken a wrong turn days before when he had dropped me off. I remembered seeing a house not too far away near where two farmers had turned us back, instructing us to take the other road.

Assured that my memory was serving me well, I decided to take the quickest way to safety. The track took me up a small winding hill and dropped down sharply on the other side before bending back towards the mountains, almost double backing on my route. I followed it for twenty minutes, always expecting the farmhouse to be around the next corner. Disappointment turned to anxiety as I began to doubt that I had made the right decision. I quickened my pace, determined to bring it all to an end. At last, by the faint glow of starlight, I made out a dark shadow dominating the clearing to my right. I thought I glimpsed a light but couldn't be sure if the stars were playing tricks on my longing weary eyes.

'It must be the house.'

I followed the track round and cut through an opening into the clearing. As I hobbled closer I was hit with the sickening feeling that I had made the wrong choice. The place was eerie and desolate, no sound, no light and no sign of life. Two huge wood panel doors bolted shut by a padlock ended my hopes. The building wasn't a house, it was a barn. I peeked through the gaps imagining a luxurious pile of hay inside. Sleep was all I could think about, it was close on four days and as many nights since I'd had any. I considered breaking in, wondering if this would be as good as it got. I could probably survive a night here, but decided I needed urgent medical help. Demoralized, I turned my back on the barn and limped back the way I came.

A weary mixture of joy and relief came over me as I reached the fork for a second time. I sensed my ordeal coming to an end and the difference between failure and making it was now only a small number of steps. Snow, trees, water and ice had been my world, an abyss from which I was slowly but surely escaping. Safety and refuge was within my grasp, all I had to do was reach out. I looked at the twinkling distant lights of Fagaras one last time before they disappeared behind the trees. The path beyond the fork levelled off and the surface steadily improved until it became something resembling a road. I had the idea in my head that the village lay no more than a mile away, so after forty minutes I expected and hoped to see a house beyond each bend. Now that walking was easy it didn't matter how far off it was, simply knowing I was nearing safety was enough to bring about an incredible revival in my physical abilities and my will to keep going. I felt strong enough to keep walking no matter how great the distance. My earlier fading strength was eclipsed by renewed verve and, as I hobbled along, I wondered how long the journey would have taken without my injuries. I figured I'd covered between 8 and 11 kilometres, which I normally could have walked in two and half hours. I fell only once, but enjoyed the moment's rest. All I needed now was some warm food, a cup of tea and a good night's sleep, everything else was superfluous.

The track grew noticeably wider as it curved into a large S-bend. Great mounds of snow had been stacked high in neat piles along both sides of the road, some sections were nearly as tall as me. Ahead to my right I saw a wooden fence sectioning off a small yard from the forest with a building visible on the far side. As I came closer I could see it was definitely a house and not a barn. I was tempted to squeeze through the gaps in the fence and cross the field straight to it, instead I pressed on along the track. Within minutes I reached a small gated path leading to the front doorway, it was only just after eight o'clock and there were no lights on. Nobody was home. I continued along the track more reassured than disappointed – there would surely be other houses with someone in. I could have moved quicker, but somehow there didn't seem to be any point. I thought how dramatic it would be to report I arrived at my last breath, fighting to the death, but although it satisfied me to know and feel that I had extra reserves, I just wanted to do this with calm and dignity. The next ten minutes were charged with anticipation and sweet thoughts – somewhere through these trees lay the village and sanctuary. I felt a surge of purpose because I knew I was going to pull it off and that I was closing in on the end. I followed a sharp bend in the track and when I came out the other side I saw a small wooden building tucked into a corner of the woods, a dilapidated old wood panel fence ran up along one side. I followed it around to the front of the house where a small gap revealed a window, a TV flashed shadows across the wall behind a man.

Just as I was taking my final steps my sock fell off, exposing my bare and frostbitten foot. I remained still and stared at it, seeing its blackness in the light emerging from the window, feeling some bizarre gratitude and strange attachment to the sock for having made it to the very end. I spoke a kind word to it and waited a few moments, shifting my attention between the sock and my exposed foot. I realized I was over-whelmed, the euphoria and relief had me caught somewhere between laughing and crying, an emotion created by intense experience. Standing alone beneath an enormous stared sky and trembling slightly, I looked myself up and down to see what was left of me – a body shattered, frozen and crushed – and I felt a strange sense of strength and power come over me. My ordeal had had a unique purity about it, a purity in the freedom of my self-rescue, throughout which I was de-tached and independent of all else. I had owned nothing, only the wind and snow on my back and it had all been down to me. I realized something obvious, yet profound: the body is nothing more than an honest and faithful tool, no more than a servant. If my consciousness could dominate it, then it would always come back to life, all I had to do was to endure. My heart was an engine, my engine, and it was more than any design or machine could ever be. Never have I felt so closely in touch with myself, suspended in those moments with my body and my heart. They were of superior stuff; they faltered, but went on. Nobody can know how proud I was.

PART TWO

Disease is an impediment to the body, but not to the will, unless the will itself chooses. Lameness is an impediment to the leg, but not to the will. And add this reflection on the occasion of everything that happens, for you will find it an impediment to something else, but not to yourself.

The Enchiridion or The Manual, Epictetus

I thought I had already experienced the limits of horror and endurance, and that I was a tough fighting man who would return home in due course with a great story of survival and be up and running again and doing what I had always done in no time at all. In my description of my experiences between the avalanche and reaching the hut I have used words and expressions to convey as vividly as possible my predicament. But I should have reserved these words for what came later, even though they are not strong enough. It is a mistake to use that kind of vocabulary without carefully weighing and measuring them, or their meaning will have been bleached out from them when one needs them later. It is a mistake for instance to use the word agony to describe a few cold nights out in the open or a couple of broken bones.

I should perhaps end my account here for my skills and powers as a writer are inadequate for what I have to tell of what followed. However, I shall try and let my memory speak as clearly as possible and do my best to put my experience onto paper.

CHAPTER ELEVEN

REFUGE

I went to pick up my sock but for some incomprehensible reason I decided to leave it where it fell. My final steps followed the fence round to the front of the house where a missing section allowed for a gateway to the door. As I was about to knock a strange thought occurred to me: what if they don't help me? I was aware that I must have looked wild and intimidating, covered in snow and blood, shoeless on one foot, and wearing torn camouflaged fatigues. Hesitating, I wondered if I should get back down on the ground so I looked less of a threat and weak enough for them to take pity on me. If I was still on my feet, they may think I was capable or even dangerous and turn me away. Dismissing my ideas I knocked on the door and waited, nobody responded so I tried again. After a moment the sound of the TV dropped and I heard footsteps coming from inside. As the door creaked open I threw my stick to the ground so as not to cause alarm.

A small old man dressed in a worn black suit stood in front of me, the primitive scent of wood smoke and the stale odour of food and booze floated out the door.

'Please help me!' I pleaded.

He looked confused and scared, nervously mumbling to himself in Romanian.

'Avalanche!' I pointed towards the mountains, hoping he would understand.

The old man looked puzzled, he didn't know what I wanted. He kept adjusting his head side to side as if examining me, he looked drunk and confused. From behind me I heard footsteps and turned to see a huge bearded man approaching aggressively with a stick in his hand.

'*Avalanşă!*' I repeated, desperate now.

As he came closer he saw my condition under the light spilling from the door, but still he remained unsure.

'Moldoveanu, *avalanşă!*' I said again.

This time he understood and communicated something to the old man who beckoned me to come in. As I reached for my stick, the big man, already suspicious and alert, grabbed his stick too and waved it aggressively in my direction. I pointed to my bad leg and made to hop forward to demonstrate my disability. He nodded as if he understood, took my stick away and put his arms under mine, lifted me with ease and carried me inside. The old man darted in front of us, pulled out a stool from under the table and placed it next to an old wood burner. I looked about the room, it was very simple: wooden walls and bare floorboards, without carpet or rugs. A table, chairs and a bed were the only furniture in the house.

In the light of the room they saw how bad a state I was in. Both men rushed about me attentively, throwing a constant barrage of questions at me which I didn't understand. It was as best as I could do to keep repeating the words '*avalanșă*' and 'Moldoveanu'. The big guy instructed the old man to bring me some clothes, while he stared at me, shaking his head and uttering words I reckoned to mean I was in trouble. It seemed a lifetime since I had last experienced indoor warmth and after only five minutes my body temperature had risen sharply from being out of the cold and I could move only in slow and floppy actions. As I defrosted, old aches and pains returned and I became extremely weak and began to sink in my chair. The old man brought over the bundle of clothes for me, but in my weakening state I just sat there like a child and let them undress me. Awkwardly, I remembered I had wet and soiled myself but didn't have the energy to try and hide it to save myself from the embarrassment. I was shocked when my vest was pulled off, I had wasted away so severely my torso was totally unrecognizable.

The old man called out urgently and started pointing to my foot, drawing his friend's attention to whatever it was that alarmed him. The big man lifted my leg for a closer look and started shaking his head again. Until then I hadn't been overly worried, I was still unable to feel anything so I hadn't paid it much attention, especially as it looked to be OK from above. Concerned and curious, I wanted to examine it but they had already set about trying to remove the boot off the other foot. When the initial effort failed, the old man gave the boot a sharp yank at the heel, causing me to scream out and grab my leg. When the pain subsided I gesticulated that it was broken and they had to be careful. The message was understood but ignored. The way that they were talking to each other told me they were serious about removing the boot. I allowed them to try again, their efforts did nothing more than send another bolt of pain shooting up my leg. I screamed more loudly and fell off my stool, ending up sprawled across the floor. I nearly started sobbing; it had felt better when I was out in the cold. With my back against the floorboards, the big guy held my leg down above the knee, while the old man tried to pull my boot off. I screamed out at the twist and pull of shifting bone. Even without its laces the boot was frozen fast and wouldn't budge an inch. I was lifted back onto the stool and the old man brought over a small wooden box, placing it close to the fire. He carefully lifted my leg and rested the boot on top of the box so that the heat from the burner could defrost my foot and the frozen boot. I was then dressed in a small cotton pyjama top that must have seen as many years as I had.

The old man brought over the remains of his meal from the table and encouraged me to eat. My earlier hunger had deserted me and it vanished altogether after I broke the pastry off the pie with my fork. Sitting beneath it was what looked like a small brain swimming in thin and unappealing-coloured gravy. The two men eyed me, nodding their heads and beckoning me to eat. I managed to force down a forkful of pastry but it tasted cold and foul. The old man was eager to point out that I had missed the meat, pointing at it with his finger. I could see they mistook my distaste for a polite reluctance to eat my host's meal and they joined together in encouraging me to eat more. Disguising my sudden loss of appetite, I cut a small slice and covered it with pastry before putting it into my mouth, managing to swallow it without retching. It was followed by a heavily prompted and disgusting second forkful, after which I pushed the plate away. They seemed satisfied that I had managed to eat something.

Next up came the vodka. A clear bottle and a shot glass were placed on the table in front of me, a more than generous measure was poured out into the glass and pushed into my hand. The large man lifted his hand to his mouth and tipped his head back, motioning for me to neck it. I took a small sip followed by a fit of coughing and spluttering. I was no drinker! The two men laughed jovially at my pathetic effort and inability to handle my spirit, and then the big man demonstrated how it was done, before adding a splash more to my glass. Downing what must have been a triple measure of neat vodka was a daunting task, a large part sprayed back out of my nose but I managed to swallow enough to receive applause, prompting the old man to slap my back in congratulations. The big guy poured another measure out, I could see by the earnest look on his face that this was more than a drinking game or guest custom; he felt there was some medicinal purpose and I was too weak to think independently or protest. I downed the measure and pushed the glass away, in truth, more out of not wanting to disappoint than being able to think straight. I was too far gone to notice the effects of drunkenness, and although my insides felt warmer, I knew it had been a mistake. What I needed was to be put on a drip, and the only thing I should have been drinking was sips of water in small quantities. It was too late now, the damage was already done.

After the eating and drinking, the men signalled it was time for another attempt at removing my boot. The old man gently lifted my leg from the box, while the big guy lifted me under my arms and lowered me onto the floor. I closed my eyes and braced myself for the agony to come; I could only hope that the vodka had numbed my senses. First, I felt the pressure of a pair of hands push the back of my knee into the floorboards, then the old man went to work on my boot, this time he was slow and gentle. I gritted my teeth at a few sharp tugs then gradually I began to feel the boot work its way free. A couple more slightly aggressive twists and it came away from my foot, pulling my sock off with it. The men positioned themselves, eager to examine the underside of my foot, giving me a welcome thumbs up to show there was nothing to worry about. It was a massive relief, as the possibility of having both feet amputated was more than I could handle in my fragile state. While I remained on the floor my worn camouflaged trousers were removed and my legs helped into a pair of pyjama bottoms. It was embarrassing wriggling around the floor trying to pull them up and, seeing my difficulty, the old man put a pair of socks on for me. Fully dressed, the big man lifted me back up onto my stool. I looked at the ridiculous bright green pyjamas I was wearing, and it wasn't difficult to imagine the old man in such an amusing outfit.

The two men then began talking and I somehow understood that the big man was leaving to find help. I nodded and sat in silence, staring into the flames. Now that I was safe and there was less activity in the room, I started to grasp the magnitude of my ordeal; the effects were more profound than I could ever have imagined. Suddenly I wanted to be alone and to cry. Sensing my distress the old man brought a stool over and sat next to me, he rubbed my shoulder in a warm friendly way as if to tell me everything was all right. The quiet was broken when his attentions were caught by my boot. Retrieving it from the spot where it came off, he examined it attentively. He was much taken by it, admiring its strength and quality. He asked me something. I was initially slow to understand before realizing that he wanted to try the boot on. The old man removed his old, worn leather worker's boots and tried mine on for size. He stood up and took a few proud strides around the room, laughing and making satisfactory remarks as he went. He stopped suddenly, looked over at me and began pointing at my feet. He wanted to know where the other boot was. He looked alarmed when he learned that I had lost it in the stream and shook his head in disbelief as I demonstrated the action with hand movements. I found myself wishing I still had the other one so I could give him the pair, which would have been the least he deserved for his care.

In no time the big guy had returned and was followed into the room by a middle-aged couple and two girls in their late teens. The small gathering stood watching me as though I were some exotic zoo animal, expecting me to do something at any second. I sat by the fire feeling awkward that so many eyes were on me and ridiculous because of the bright green seventies pyjamas I was now dressed in. After the initial silence and staring came the introductions, each person in turn walked over, shook my hand and told me their name. The two young girls offered me their cheeks to kiss and politely kissed my blood-stained cheeks back. When everyone was done I introduced myself, they all repeated my name and the room returned to silence. Taking the lead the big guy pointed to himself and the others and said, 'Romania.' Next he pointed to me.

'England,' I replied.

My response was met with excited whispers. A torrent of questions followed, none of which I understood. Bemused, I gave the answers of 'Moldoveanu' and '*avalanşă*' wherever I thought applicable. One of the girls asked me if I could understand French but we were unable to make much progress as her French was worse than mine, and every other word was excitedly interrupted for translation. The girl told me that there was a boy in the village who could speak some English; she would go and fetch him. As the girls were hurried out the door, I called out after them: 'Chocolate . . . Coca Cola.' These universals needed no translation. I removed the waterproofed bank notes from my jungle trousers and handed some over.

A brief inactivity followed their departure. While those who remained talked in cautionary whispers, I took the chance to take a look at my frostbite. I removed the sock and turned the underside of my foot up, seeing that the entire sole was hard and black. There was no pain and it felt dead and devoid of any sensation. I tapped at the ball of my foot with my fingernail, then with a knife from the table. It made a solid sound, as though I was banging the knife against a piece of wood. Slowly, I ran my finger from the tips of my big toe down to the heel searching for any sense of touch but there was nothing. I only felt life where the line of blackness gave way to cold pink skin.

After fifteen minutes the girls returned without the boy, saying he would arrive shortly. In the meantime she gave me a bar of Cadbury's Dairy Milk chocolate and a 2-litre bottle of Seven-Up. The girls refused to keep the change so I decided I would use it to buy chocolate for everyone when the English-speaking boy arrived. My desire to drink was great. I dreamily anticipated the sensation of the sweet fizzy drink on my tongue and running down my throat, after all, I'd been promising myself this for so long. The girl brought a glass and the bottle over, but seeing I was too weak to unscrew the cap off she did it herself and filled my glass. I offered the bottle around but nobody accepted. I gulped the first mouthful greedily but the taste was foul, the inside of my mouth had become so dry and disgusting that it polluted the sweetness of the drink. I was hardly able to swallow and my throat felt uncomfortably tight, as though the sides would crack or burn away. I tried to gulp down a few mouthfuls but my stomach couldn't handle the gas. I began to feel drowsy and could sense the beginnings of a dull ache in my stomach. My body wasn't taking kindly to the accelerated warming up, nor to the vodka and fizzy drinks. I signalled that I couldn't drink any more and requested water instead. The crowd of faces surrounding me looked concerned. My inability to drink prompted one of the girls to unwrap the bar of chocolate, break it up into squares and place one in my hands. The chocolate felt as though it would break my teeth and I couldn't taste anything, it was like having a plastic Lego block inside my mouth. I could manage no more than two squares so insisted it was shared out. Reluctantly they all took a piece, but as with the vodka, I think it was just out of politeness. When I'd finished eating, one of the girls came to my side, and like a mother with her child, began to clean my face with a wet tissue. I couldn't believe the dirt and dried blood that came off.

A knock came at the door and the teenage boy who let himself in was greeted warmly by the old man and directed straight towards me. One of the girls offered him a square of the chocolate and introduced me.

'Hello, my friend, my name is Bogdan. I am here to help you,' he said.

I thanked him and prepared myself for the inevitable questions as he sat his stool next to mine and hit me with his first.

'Manchester United? Leeverpool?'

I smiled and shook my head, and when I replied 'Arsenal' all the men made a sigh of disappointment. A round of naming British footballers followed.

'Ryan Giggs, David Beckham, Alan Shear-ha . . .'

Out of courtesy I felt it only fair to name-drop some Romanian players too. 'Gheorghe Hagi, Raducioiu, Mutu, Dan Petrescu.'

The men were pleasantly surprised. Next came the real questions about my accident, and with each answer they looked more intrigued. There were many interruptions and enquiries came thick and fast, causing the boy to become lost in the cross fire of translation. A brief silence preceded the ultimate question, 'How did you get here?'

All eyes were fixed on me as I replied, 'I crawled back.'

'You crawled off the mountain for three days?' Bogdan double-checked.

After he translated the room was flooded in an almost embarrassing complete silence. The big man walked over to me, said something serious and held out his hand for me to shake.

'You are a man my friend,' Bogdan translated. Laughing, he added, 'You cannot drink but you are still a man.'

The old man joined in too and came over to shake my hand. After clearing up a few more details such as where my boot had gone and what I had eaten, the questions moved on to easier subject matter. They were interested to know why I had chosen to visit their country and they seemed very proud and honoured that I had done so. Specifically they wanted to know what I thought of Bucharest, Brasov, the mountains, the people, the food and the girls. I mostly gave truthful answers, but chose to lie about Bucharest. I said that I had liked it very much and that the city reminded me of Paris.

After about an hour in the old man's hut, a powerful weariness took hold of me. My body temperature had skyrocketed and the new levels of warmth seemed to be thawing out all the damage that had been frozen away on the slopes. A horribly uncomfortable sensation of aches and dizziness that gripped my body came upon me quite suddenly. I continued answering their questions as best as I could until my head started to pulsate and my focus began to fade. I no longer possessed the energy to contend with people or questions, my eyelids were opening and shutting uncontrollably and I needed sleep. Out of nowhere, I was asked something by the big guy that I didn't immediately understand, he was pointing to one of the girls. The girl looked at me and smiled. Bogdan intervened, 'She likes you and she said you are beautiful. Do you like her? She wants to know.'

All eyes were expectantly upon me. I deliberately said I liked everyone, as though I had misunderstood the question, but they looked disappointed. I wondered if I should say something else as maybe they'd only been joking; the girl couldn't possibly like someone who looked so awful.

'She wants to be your girlfriend,' Bogdan shouted excitedly.

Close to passing out, I slid from the stool and eyed the old man's bed at the far end of the room. People rushed forward to help me up but I was already on my way, crawling again, this time across wooden floorboards instead of snow, my mind and body totally dominated by the urge to sleep. As I reached the bed, one of the girls came over to help me up and pulled the covers back. Panting and delirious with exhaustion, I flopped down onto the mattress and wriggled my way across the bed. Before I pulled my head beneath the covers I caught a glimpse of the poor old man's face. 'The cheek of it,' he must have thought as I submerged beneath the woollen blankets into a world of warmth and darkness. My head was going round and round and I felt mind-numbingly drunk. Blankets were piled on top of me while the bed swayed like a hammock and the whole house seemed to spin. The voices died down and all I could hear was the crackle of firewood.

I woke without knowing where I was but was quick to recognize that my condition had worsened drastically. I had become very cold and had started shivering violently, an unrelenting ache flowed through my body, causing me to shift about in search for some comfortable position to fight away the pain. I was losing control of my body much more than at any time on the mountain. It felt wrong that this should be happening to me now; I had thought that making it back was the end of it all. Bogdan sat on the bed and placed a hand on my shoulder, he proudly showed me his mobile phone.

'Do you want me to call the ambulance?'

I told him I needed help urgently.

CHAPTER TWELVE

THE ORDEAL BEGINS

The next thing I remember was the murmur of voices and the flash of blue and red lights streaming through the window and dancing up against the back wall and ceiling. Still caught in the maelstrom of deep pain, exhaustion and confusion, I had the strangest sensation of being in a nightmare: I didn't know where I was, lights hit my eyes, and mysterious people around me spoke in a language I didn't understand. I wondered if I was awake or asleep or even dead or alive.

After questioning Bogdan about my condition and what had happened to me, I was lifted out of the old man's bed and laid onto a stretcher by two paramedics. They didn't waste time examining me, and sensing I was in no state to answer questions, wrapped me in a heavy blanket and wheeled me out to an ambulance. The instant I left the warmth of the house I was brought to by an icy cold blast against my face and exposed arms. I knew straight away that I wouldn't have lasted another night out in these conditions and wondered how I'd got through any at all. There was little room in the back of the vehicle but Bogdan managed to convince the medics his translation skills would be required. Everyone came out to say goodbye: the men shook my hand and the women kissed my cheek. The girl who had brought me chocolate stroked my hair and pulled the blanket up under my chin before kissing my forehead and saying goodbye and good luck in English. I stammered through my emotional farewell as Bogdan translated for me.

The ambulance looked like the *Ghostbusters'* van and seemed comical given my circumstances. Inside, one of the stretcher runners was higher on one side than the other. I had to push against the wall of the vehicle with an outstretched arm to stop myself tipping out. The roads were snow-clogged, bumpy and full of potholes, all the ingredients for an uncomfortable journey. I suddenly felt alone, and even though Bogdan was at my side, I was hit with a sense of dread at what was coming. I'd thought that a good night's sleep and a warm meal were all I needed, now I realized things were far more serious and uncertain. For the first time it occurred to me that this might only be the beginning, not the end of my troubles.

Within half an hour we reached the hospital and the first thing I saw when the rear doors were opened was an illuminated stone archway with a cross on top. It looked like a small church; I had been brought to a chapel hospice. Once inside, nurses ran to help me and I was wheeled into a small, warm and brightly lit room and transferred onto a hospital bed. There were no doctors, three nurses wearing crucifixes attended to me carrying out basic checks, cleaning the filth off my face and hands and dressing me in a clean hospital gown. A nurse brought in a cup of warm sugary tea and a bowl of small bread pieces soaked in warm milk. She started to spoon feed me, bringing the tea to my mouth between each piece of bread. When I only managed two or three squares the nurses looked concerned. They forced me to drink more of the tea, even though most of it went down my chin. I felt worse for having something in me, my body simply didn't have the energy to digest food. I needed direct intravenous fluids, which I tried to explain by pointing to my veins. The ordeal was catching up with me, my body reacting to the trauma I had inflicted upon it.

The nurses left the room and called Bogdan to follow them. I was alone again and lay on the bed staring at the yellow walls wondering how all this would end. My stomach moved and I remembered the attack that had hit me hours before on the track. Moments later it returned in full force, a torturous spasm coming from deep within my guts. I arched my back and screamed out in roaring agony. My stomach contracted further and the pain increased, making me cry out in the most unimaginable and terrifying pain. The nurses came rushing back in at the commotion but didn't seem to know what to do. I howled out a litany of obscenities in utter despair, willing someone to do something to help me. When I could scream no more, I broke into weak desperate sobs. The nurses were talking to me, with Bogdan doing his best to translate, but in the midst of my crisis nothing became any clearer. For a few forgiving seconds the pain stopped, then started up again and again, getting worse each time. My body writhed and convulsed so much that I would have thrown myself off the bed had the nurses and ambulance men not caught me. One of them lifted the rails up on the sides of the bed and tried to hold me down. My arms broke free and flew wildly, knocking over the bedside cabinet and sending the bowl of milk with bread crashing to the floor. I was pinned down again, gripped at each limb, and when the pain subsided I was rushed outside, loaded back into the ambulance and strapped down. Within twenty minutes we reached a second hospital, where a doctor and his staff rushed out to meet us. It took all of two minutes to decide they didn't have the facilities to treat me and that they didn't want to take responsibility if anything went wrong. We would have to go to the city hospital in Brasov, a three-hour journey by road. The ambulance crew must have worried I wasn't going to make it because they drove like maniacs along roads that were covered in snow and ice. It was a terrible journey during which, between stomach attacks, I was thrown over the sides of the stretcher and had to be lifted back in again. The driver ignored my cries and concentrated on the road while Bogdan continually reassured me. We made Brasov in less than two hours, in what must have been record time.

A whole team of medical staff rushed out to the ambulance at the doors of the city hospital and, following a blur of activity, I found myself alone in a corridor. A female doctor who spoke good English brought me a telephone so I could call home. I ignored the request as I didn't want my mother to know and be upset, but the doctor was insistent and stayed watching over me. My dad answered. I told him I had broken my leg and had missed my flight but I would organize something soon. I felt content to have got rid of the thoughts of family from my mind and the emotions associated with them. Maybe it was selfish but I was only able to concentrate on myself. I especially couldn't handle my mother's inevitable distress. The sense of urgency had died down as I was no longer screaming and I was moved to a small ward, where Bogdan sat beside me trying his best to make conversation with talk of football. Within half an hour a doctor was at my bedside, the consultation was well timed, coinciding with another stomach attack, only worse and more prolonged than any of the previous ones. I thrashed around the bed, screaming, shouting out obscenities and bursting into crying fits in between calls for help. Bogdan and the doctor tried to hold onto me, but without intending to I was striking them in my agony induced fit. A team of nurses rushed in and took hold of my limbs, but still they were unable to contain me. The doctor questioned me urgently, but I wasn't listening to anything he said, I just wanted him to act.

'Help, give me some morphine!' I screamed repeatedly.

When he didn't respond I swore at him, then reverted to begging when the insults didn't work.

'Where is the pain? Where is it coming from?' the doctor kept asking me while I kept shouting for morphine.

It took until the beat of pain dropped a notch for me to whimper a response, 'My stomach. Please give me some morphine.'

He wanted me to show him. I lifted my pyjama top and touched the source of the pain with my fingers. He pressed his fingers forcefully into my belly as if trying to feel for something.

'Kenneth, I am going to operate on you, do you understand? I will cut you open and look inside your stomach.'

I didn't care, as long as the pain was gone, anything. I agreed, still repeating my demands for morphine; this time he said I could have it. The pain started up again and I thrashed around the bed for some minutes before an anaesthetist came. It took several nurses, the doctor and Bogdan to hold me down. I watched in pleasure as the hypodermic needle was brought down towards me and I welcomed it in. The dizzy and fading sensation quickly came upon me as the faces holding me down became blurred and turned purple. I had no fear of death, and if this was my farewell to life, the escape from such agony made it a sweet and blissful exit.

When my eyelids fluttered I saw a nurse looking down on me and felt my hand being squeezed. I didn't know how long I'd been under for, and had no idea of the time, or whether it was night or day. The only thing I really noticed was that my body reeked of disinfectant, I must have been given a thorough cleaning before they operated on me, but still they hadn't been able to fully remove the filth ground into my hands and beneath my fingernails. I didn't observe much else as the hours passed in fits and bursts of intermittent awakening and returns to the abandonment of sleep. The first I knew of coming round properly was my consternation at seeing eight lines running from a drip stand into my arms. I was horrified, I'd trained as a combat medic and knew that eight drips was bad. As I became more awake my breathing became difficult. My stomach pulled my chest painfully tight, so that I dared not take a deep breath. Being careful not to disturb the drips, I slowly pulled the covers back and explored my torso. I couldn't move my neck into the right angle to see well enough so I sent my hand down and encountered what I thought was a drip line. I forced my neck down and saw four thick tubes running into my stomach. A large white bandage over ten inches long covered the centre line of my torso. Distraught, I pulled the covers back over me and fell into a drowsy sleep.

When I next woke, a doctor wearing a white coat stood at the end of my bed.

'Kenneth, do you believe in God?' he asked. 'Because it is a miracle you are still here. I have never seen anyone with so many injuries still alive.'

I remained silent, too confused to care or answer. I couldn't remember if this was the same doctor who had told me he would operate. After his exclamations the doctor went on to describe the cause of my pain and the surgery he had carried out. Stress-induced ulcers in my stomach had perforated and started haemorrhaging blood and gastric acid, so he had cut the perforated areas out and repaired the holes. He said he'd given me at best a 30 per cent chance of surviving. To understand the causes of my condition he wanted to know what had happened to me. Until that moment I had forgotten about my leg, telling the doctor how I had dragged myself off the mountain reminded me. Moving away from my story I asked about the break, if it was bad and how soon I would be up and walking again. The doctor's grave expression gave away his answer.

'I'm afraid it's unlikely you will walk again. The fall from the cliff shattered your pelvis and the femoral head broke with it. The injury is massive and probably irreparable.'

He went on, telling me I would need extensive treatment and reminding me how lucky I was to be alive. My initial emotion was rage, but the feeling was quickly cloaked by immense sadness. Words had never hit me so hard, so I deluded myself into believing the message had been lost in translation, even though the doctor clearly spoke good English. The news got worse, the frostbite to my foot was deep and if it didn't improve quickly then they would have to amputate. He said they would have already removed it if it weren't for the risk of infection and the urgent situation with my stomach taking priority. My head throbbed at the impact of everything I was being told, I tried to protest but my interruptions fell on deaf ears.

'Remember, you should be dead,' he kept telling me.

The doctor couldn't understand that I didn't give a damn how fortunate I was. I just wanted to hear that I would be OK and that I would be able to walk again. I threw more futile questions at him, looking for answers I wasn't going to find. When I'd tired of putting up resistance he told me it was necessary to put my leg in traction and I was to press the red button if the pain returned. After the doctor had gone I was left alone and prey to my thoughts. I was devastated and sickened, after everything that had happened this was how I had ended up, condemned to my bed, riddled with pipes and never to walk again. On the mountain it had been so simple and uncomplicated; it had all been down to me. Now my fate was out of my hands. I would definitely lose the possibility of rejoining the army, and university would probably be over too. I had never felt so useless in my life and began to wish I had died on the mountain. As I drifted into sleep my mind flashed back to a picture I'd seen in Stirling Lines, the SAS base in Hereford, during my interview for a place on Selection. The upper half of the image was of the famous 'Who Dares Wins' winged-dagger cap badge with 'One day cock of the farmyard' written in an arc above it. The bottom half of the picture showed the cap badge turned upside down so that it looked more like a dusting brush, with the inscription 'next day feather duster' written beneath. I suddenly felt as though I was finished.

When I woke again my earlier depression had been forgotten and replaced by an interest in re-tuning my body clock. I still had no idea whether it was day or night and couldn't for the life of me tell how many hours or days had passed. Seeing me awake, a nurse came over to my bed informing me I had a visitor. A dark-skinned man with closely cropped hair was shown to my bay and the nurse accompanying him left us alone. He spoke good English and introduced himself as a detective here to investigate my accident. He opened his enquiry by informing he had already spoken to Bogdan, before taking out a notepad and recording the particulars of my home life and details of my trip: why I had come to Romania, if I was travelling alone, etc. When satisfied, he got down to the bones of his case.

'Tell me what happened to you on the mountain,' he said. 'How were your injuries caused? Was there somebody else with you? Did someone push you?'

I explained I was on my own but the answer was met with resistance.

'So you didn't have an argument or a fight with anybody who then pushed you?'

The question seemed like a double negative and still caught in the haze of anaesthesia, I began to wonder if someone had been with me and that maybe I had been pushed after all. Perhaps I hadn't seen them or lost my memory after the fall.

'No, nobody pushed me, I was on my own,' I answered finally.

The pause to search my mind for the truth aroused his suspicions further.

'You're sure you didn't have an argument or a fight with anyone?'

'No, I told you: there was an avalanche, I ran, it hit me and I fell.'

211

'And when did this happen?'

Before I was able to answer he offered me a scenario.

'You had a fight on the mountain . . . you were pushed . . . then they had to carry you back to the village. Then they left because they thought they would have trouble. You don't need to worry, if somebody pushed you, we will find him.'

I asked the detective the time and day so that I could get my facts right and set about telling him what had happened and how I got off the mountain. He did as detectives do, prompting me regularly and asking a lot of questions. Halfway through I noticed he had stopped taking notes but still encouraged me to keep talking. He was the first person to hear a full account of what happened to me and I think he enjoyed it. After he left, my drips were changed and I was administered a dose of morphine. The pain vanished, my heart rate slowed down and my body seemed to sink into the mattress. I wasn't lonely any more and even the possibility of not walking again didn't arouse any sentiments, it was just an idea that could no longer trouble me. Morphine is miraculous, and soon sleep would temporarily eclipse everything.

I was awoken by the loud wail of an emotional woman and the sound of nurses running past my bed to the end of the small ward. I found out later that her husband was dying. Staring at the grey walls, I listened sadly to her desperate sobs and the noise of rain against the window panes. It pelted the glass with a steady rhythm and the sky outside looked miserable and grey. There was nothing there to comfort the human heart and, unable to take much more I returned beneath the blankets, too scared to wake fully and commit myself to the suffering and uncertainty of another day. Soon after, the pain made its customary return, creeping upon me subtly until I was unable to move any part of my body without it getting worse. Too confused to remember the red button, I stayed silent and listened to my faint breath, simply waiting for something to happen, to hear some news, anything. Eventually two nurses came to my bed and carried out a multitude of checks: blood pressure, temperature and a blood sample, then drained the bags connected to my stomach. Seeing all the pipes going into me made me feel like a dying man. They gave me more intravenous drugs, the pain quickly subsided and I immediately felt better.

After they were done, another nurse came to my bed, but she looked more like a nun in her black robe-like uniform. As she began treating my frostbite I craned my neck eagerly to see what she would do. After a gentle clean she painted the entire foot in iodine, leaving it an orangey-brown colour, then re-bandaged it. She worked quickly and looked as though she had dealt with such things before. The nurse said something I gathered to be a kind word and left me. Alone again, I thought about food. I hadn't eaten anything in nearly a week and wondered why I wasn't hungry. I pressed the buzzer and a nurse came immediately. I asked for something to eat but she shook her head with a sympathetic smile, indicating that my food was in the drips. I returned my gaze to the pattern of rain splattering against the window and within minutes I was asleep.

I woke again with the familiar sensations of loneliness, confusion and creeping pain. Not knowing how long I would have to be in the hospital was the worst thing and I found myself wishing someone could be with me, the uncertainty of it all was as traumatizing as my injuries. I considered ringing the buzzer, anticipating that the pain would quickly become unbearable, but really it was for the company of a nurse. As tears welled up in my eyes for no reason, I looked across the ward and saw my mum and dad walking towards my bed. Never had I felt such overwhelming relief and joy to see my family, but when I saw how upset my mother was I began to feel a deep sense of remorse that she had to see me like this. She held me tightly and kissed my head, tears streaming down her face, then sat on my bed and broke into a story of overseas phone calls and the nightmare journey to Romania. My dad hadn't believed a word of my broken-leg story and was straight back on the phone to the hospital. The surgeon they spoke to had told them how close a call it had been, which he had reiterated before they entered the ward. Hearing of my trauma, my mother knew that something terrible must have happened and wanted me to tell her everything. Despite my efforts to conceal the worst parts, there were too many questions to cover up the truth. In the end, she heard everything: the avalanche and the fall from the cliff, the lost equipment, the crawl off the mountain and through the forest, the freezing nights in the open, stream crossings, reaching the old man's hut and the sequence of ambulance journeys to different hospitals that ended here in Brasov.

When the nurses next came to carry out their scheduled checks my mum saw for the first time all the lines going into both arms and the tubes leading into my stomach. Clearly shocked, I tried to distract her by cracking a few jokes and felt a little better when I saw her smile. After the nurses left I told her I'd forgotten exactly what the surgeon had done to me and asked her to remind me. She explained the procedure that had been carried out and why I was in so much pain. A ten-inch vertical incision had been made straight through my stomach muscle, which was now held together by giant Frankenstein-like stitches. My mum told me there was no worse pain than perforated ulcers, which stirred a memory of what a sadistic instructor had told my platoon in the Paras.

'Don't get shot in the stomach, it's the most painful way to die.'

According to the surgeon I had made it just in time – had they not operated on me immediately I would have been dead.

The remainder of the day was a blur of medical checks, falling in and out of sleep and answering more questions from my mum about the fall and the details of my journey back. Exhausted, and my mind still clouded by the effects of drugs, I became obsessed with knowing the time because it reassured me to be certain about something. No matter how often I was told, I quickly forgot or suffered an inability to gauge how much time has passed since my last enquiry. My dad showed indefatigable patience in telling me again and again. The day's final morphine dose was administered just before lights out and it took effect immediately. I could still feel the pain beat at my nerve endings in strange convulsions that pulsed through my stomach, but the drugs had given me a temporary immunity and the attack was deadened to a dull thud. Throughout the brief window of being pain-free I felt a renewed energy and enthusiasm to talk. I told my parents that the surgeon had said I might never be able to walk again, but their quiet reassurances calmed me, convincing me that somebody back home would be able to do something.

On the third day my dad took a room in a private lodging so he could get some rest, but my mum stayed at my bedside. As on previous nights, I was still awake when the effects of the morphine wore off and stayed that way until morning. Attempts to ignore the pain were always futile. I would shut my eyes and try to force myself to sleep, struggling to understand how I could be so tired, yet so incapable of something my body needed so badly. Eventually I realized I'd never been able to sleep on my back and the tubes running into my stomach prevented me from rolling over. My arms had also become increasingly weak and ached to distraction from the intrusion of having so many cannulas running into my veins. Soon these minor discomforts became completely irrelevant as the morphine wore off. Within a few hours the pain morphed into agony, and being unable to adjust my body position made it worse. I just had to lie there and let the pain steamroll over me. It was hell and all I could do was count the minutes and hours until the next dose of drugs. Waiting for morphine was like a difficult boxing fight, trying to survive until the bell, hanging on in there while getting slaughtered.

The following days continued to pass in the familiar blur of pain and sleeplessness. As soon as I received my dose of morphine, all my efforts were concentrated into falling asleep as quickly as possible, but I was so focused upon something that should have come naturally that it usually had the reverse effect. It racked me to want and need something so badly, yet to find it beyond my capabilities. Convinced I had forgotten some lost procedure or technique, I cajoled my mind into trying to recall how I normally went about going to sleep. Throughout my torment my mother remained by my side, resisting my pleas that she should go and get some rest.

On the morning of the fourth day, after all my normal checks and morphine dose, I watched in horror as a doctor pulled back the bed sheets and hammered a long thin nail into my shin bone just below my knee. Doped and caught in a half-state of sleep, I wasn't sure if what I was seeing was actually happening. After the nail came through, a pulley system was secured to the end of my bed, connected to the nail with a cord and then loaded with weights. My leg was now in traction. For the first few hours it was bearable, but it wasn't long before the device made my life hell. The constant pressure caused me to slide down the bed and pulled agonizingly at my heavily stitched stomach muscles. Any semblance of comfort disappeared and the already remote possibility of sleep was totally eliminated.

As the days passed I became more and more exhausted. My body weakened and my physical and mental resistance to the stress I was under rapidly came undone. Going without real sleep is harrowing, the body breaks down and all sense of time, place and events mean nothing. I would consider myself lucky if I caught two hours' sleep in twenty-four. The nights were the worst, the pain felt more intense with less activity to distract my mind and they were the longest periods between morphine doses. The throbbing in my stomach was so strong that it beat like a drum, attacking me in an unrelenting and pulsating rhythm. I was reduced to the desperate level of begging my mother to ask the nurses for more morphine. My depths of despair hit an all-time low when she told me that my dosage was gradually being reduced to eliminate the risk of dependency. If there was a button I could have pushed to end it all I would have done. My resilience and spirit completely snapped the day my allocation was stopped altogether. Although I was administered alternative pain relief, it was largely ineffective. I expended so much energy groaning in agony that I would intermittently succumb to sleep. Each time I woke I was obsessed with knowing how long I'd been out and even tried counting sheep in my desperate bid to return to sleep. After eight days of being drip fed my body weight had plummeted by five stone. I no longer recognized my own face in the mirror and my body looked as though it belonged to someone else. My hands curled and flopped pathetically at the wrists, becoming such useless appendages that I couldn't even scratch an itch. I was caught up in a maze of drips, pipes and traction cord; attempting the simplest things turned into a massive effort. All I yearned for was to be free of pain and to sleep; my future health was of secondary interest.

By the end of the first week I was transferred from the ward into a private room. I was briefly left alone for the first time and took the opportunity to remove my leg from traction. With one weak arm I took the tension off the pulley and with the other I loosened the cord from the nail in my shin. I could feel strange contractions as muscle and broken bones adjusted. Slowly, I allowed the remaining length of cord to run through my fingers before releasing it, sending the iron weights crashing to the ground at the end of my bed. It was the first time I had seen my legs since I had set off to climb the mountain. It was a disturbing sight, the muscles had atrophied at an astonishing rate and all the colour had faded; they looked almost skeletal. I pulled the blankets over me and flopped back onto the bed with a huge sigh. Releasing my broken joints was every bit as blissful as a dose of morphine. Despite the efforts of the staff and my mother to persuade me I remained stubborn, and no effort was made to reattach the weights. Although the nail was still in my leg, I felt as close to comfortable as I had done at any time in the hospital and was even able to sleep.

News of my ordeal and survival had by now reached the British press and it was becoming increasingly difficult to hold off the journalists and their photographers who had set up camp in the hospital's waiting area and corridors. Savvy reporters had already contacted the history department at my university and were now asking a lot of questions of hospital staff, who carried in notes addressed to me offering money for my exclusive story. My mum and dad were also besieged by reporters every time they left or entered the ward. The whole episode was embarrassing – to think that such a fuss could be made over something nobody really knew anything about. At this time I didn't feel like talking to anyone and hadn't considered that I had a story to tell. My main concern was keeping my military background out of public knowledge, especially given the nature of my previous employment. My dad kept the journalists at bay and instructed my family back home to draw all the curtains and remove any photographs of me in uniform hanging from the walls.

It took just under two weeks before my condition showed signs of improvement. I was advised to remain under observation for a further four days, after which I would be fit for travel and able to return to the UK. Despite concerns about my long-term health, I started to feel more upbeat and optimistic that all would turn out well, regardless of what the doctors had said. I knew even then that I wouldn't have made it through the nights without my mother at my bedside. My dad played his part in a different way; his hard work and positive outlook were by far his finest hours as a father.

A couple of days passed in relative comfort: I slept regularly and was permitted to eat for the first time, even though it was nothing more than two teaspoons of yoghurt and a few thin slices of banana. My morale was boosted by phone calls from my siblings, and friends from the army and university. My dad had collected my belongings from the hostel and developed the film from my disposable cameras. I was very excited to see if one of them contained the photo of the bear. The clothes I had worn on the mountain had also somehow made their way back to me. They had been washed, folded neatly and placed into a black plastic bag before being handed over to my mother. I was glad to be reunited with them and enthusiastically explained to my mother how the jacket had saved my life.

The next day I told my story again, this time to a journalist for the *Mail on Sunday*. With some creative and careful side-stepping of questions I was able to keep my military background a secret. In the end I decided I would tell part of my story as the papers back home were already making up their own version of events. The journalist was actually very useful in tying up a few loose ends and filling in gaps in my memory. I was able to learn the name of the village I had crawled back to and discovered that mountain rescue hadn't conducted a search for me in spite of all the newspapers reporting to the contrary. Apart from a couple of people I'd spoken to at the hostel and the receptionist, nobody had known I was missing, and even then they weren't sure whether or not to raise the alarm. There was also news of Bogdan and the old man: Bogdan had sold his story, telling how he'd found me lying face down in the snow wearing only a T-shirt and jeans and how he dragged me off the mountain after dressing me in his own clothes. I liked Bogdan's version, he deserved his glory. I only hoped he got a good payout as a reward for his imagination. The old man also got his moment of fame too, posing for a local newspaper outside his home with my boot in his hand. I promised myself that one day I'd be back to give him a pair of the best boots money could buy.

Now that I was more or less pain free I became excited and impatient. I hadn't seen anything beyond four grey hospital walls for two weeks and was looking forward to a change of scenery, even if it was just another hospital. The biggest discomfort was contending with my constant hunger, ten days of being drip-fed had wasted me savagely and I was still only allowed soft foods in the smallest quantities. I once managed to trick chocolate off a journalist, but after that my dad raised his level of vigilance. Things got so desperate that I found myself pleading with my mother to describe the taste of a yoghurt she was eating. She thought I was joking and became upset when she realized I was serious. I persisted until she gave in and I fooled myself I could taste her words. After this my parents wouldn't eat in front of me or tell me when they were going for a meal. For the remainder of my time in Brasov food was never discussed.

The administrative procedure to get me home proved to be a nightmare and my dad was fully occupied filling out paperwork, making phone calls and jumping over bureaucratic hurdles. It took him several days to obtain all the papers and signatures, and on the Tuesday plans were finalized for us to fly home the next day. However, Wednesday's travel plans were scuppered by bureaucracy, leaving me with yet another day in hospital while my dad made another journey to Bucharest. My mother and I sat watching the cell phone all morning, waiting to hear news of when we could all return home. I read the English newspapers left by news crews and journalists while my mother got some sleep. After two weeks she was physically and emotionally wrecked, what she had done was a staggering feat of endurance.

By midday my health took a sudden and unexpected turn for the worse. It started with unusual contractions in my lower stomach and soon after I felt light-headed. I thought I had messed myself now that I was eating small amounts but the nurse on cleaning duties discovered that I had excreted a pool of blood clots. She quickly raised the alarm, but the doctors decided it was quite normal and nothing more than my body ridding itself of waste fluid from the surgery. The contractions came and went, leaving me dizzy and confused, but not in any real pain. An hour or so later my bed sheets turned red. There was no rush of doctors this time, just the one came, instructing a nurse to give me an enema and also advising us to put our flights on hold. Fifteen minutes later the nurses found the bed pan contained a lot of blood and it continued to pour out even after the pipe had been removed. I didn't realize how bad it was until the sheets and blankets were pulled away, revealing my blood splattered legs and ankles. Suddenly things turned urgent and a team of medical staff rushed to my bed. Electrical devices were attached to me and the pipes running into my stomach were disconnected from their bags and clamped off at the ends. My head began to fade, I was losing consciousness. Scared, I called out to my mum, 'Something's happening to me.'

I could feel myself slipping away and was struggling to breathe. An oxygen mask was attached to my face.

'Breathe!' I heard my mother scream.

A few short breaths later and I was revived. I was a bit embarrassed at my panic, but even though I wasn't in pain I felt as close to dying as I imagined was possible. The team of doctors and nurses still ran frantically around me. I sat uselessly, totally unable to do anything to help myself. I stared into the mirror positioned at the end of the bed, looking at my face and into my own eyes. My reflection gave me a strange sense of reassurance that I was still here and alive.

My dad called the cell phone right on time, he was just checking all was OK before he paid the £5,000 non-refundable airline fee.

'Cancel everything and return to Brasov immediately,' I heard my mother cry.

The anaesthetist arrived and a male nurse lifted me upright in the bed so she could access my brachial artery high on my chest beneath my collar bone. A large cannula was inserted and linked up to yet another drip, and I knew then I must have lost a lot of blood. My mother's hysterical screams got closer as she forced her way back to the bedside. She pulled the anaesthetist to one side and out of my sight.

'Is he going to make it?'

I strained my ears to listen amid the activity going on around me and watched them through the mirror's reflection at the end of the bed. I saw the anaesthetist shake her head and mouth, 'I'm sorry,' then put her arms round my mother.

Neither of them knew I had seen. The sadness was immense; to see my mother's face as she was told I would die broke my heart.

There was a clank as the rails on one side of my bed were dropped. The medical staff parted and a male nurse wearing red scrubs came up to the bed.

'This is going to hurt,' he said.

He then lifted me clean off the bed. I groaned in agony as my body folded into a V-shape, broken bones shifted and the stitches holding my stomach together felt as though they were being ripped apart. He walked fast through a maze of white-tiled corridors as a team of nurses ran alongside holding my drips. The ease at which he was able to pick me up and carry me shocked me, I must have felt like a feather to him. I could still hear my mother wailing as she followed behind. I forced my neck over his shoulder and put on a brave voice, 'Don't worry, Mum, I'll be all right.'

When we started to climb the stairs I realized this was too much of an emergency to even wait for the lift. All the while the male nurse was talking to me, telling me not to worry and that I would be fine. He must have seen the fear in my face as I clung on to him tightly. Rushed into a room full of equipment, I was gently lowered down onto a surgical table. My drips were hooked up and the sheet wrapped around me was removed, leaving me naked from the waist down. A screen was positioned at one end of the room, below it was some sort of X-ray chamber. I was lifted at the waist so that support blocks could be placed under my hips to elevate my lower half. The surgeon told me they were going to look inside me to discover the origin of the bleeding. A camera on the end of a metal cable was inserted into my rectum and manoeuvred forcefully until in position. I called out in pain and jolted my legs while the man in red scrubs still supported me from behind with his arms under mine. As images came up on the screen, one of the doctors called out when he found the source of the haemorrhage. He told me it would be necessary to operate immediately. I was surprised when they asked if I agreed, I guessed they hadn't reckoned much on my chances of pulling through. Without delay I was transferred onto a stretcher bed and wheeled directly to theatre, where they told me I would see my mother after the operation. The word 'after' pleased me, I was paying close attention to everything they said. I asked a nurse to tell my mum I was feeling better, insisting upon it until she agreed she would do so. Out of nowhere, I remembered I should have been mid-flight at this exact time, probably bleeding to death. Saved by Romanian bureaucracy, that was something!

A peculiar sense of calm came over me as I lay on the operating table: I would soon be put to sleep and know no more about it; one way or another the suffering would come to an end. I watched carefully as I was anaesthetized, keeping vigilant and alert. Bright lights shone in my eyes and then the faces around me began to fade. Aware that these might be my final seconds of life, I wanted to say something and managed to murmur some words, 'Do your best.'

CHAPTER THIRTEEN

HARD TIME

I was in theatre for six and half hours and for an additional forty-eight hours I remembered nothing. It was found that the previous surgery had been unsuccessful, the stomach ulcers had haemorrhaged massively and were beyond repair. As a result two thirds of my stomach had now been removed along with my duodenum, which was switched with my small intestine and connected to the remainder of my stomach. Post operation, the surgeon told my parents I would unlikely survive twenty-four hours, and that he would be surprised if I lasted twelve. My mother tells me she sat at my bed with the anaesthetist, stroking my hair and crying until I came round three hours later. When I did I was groggy and semi-conscious, not even aware of the massive trauma I had undergone. When I fully emerged from the effects of anaesthesia, I felt OK. I wanted to know the time, the football scores and even tried to use a drip tube connected to my arm to lasso an out of reach piece of chocolate to within my grasp. When the surgeon visited my bed he smiled, shook his head and said, 'I can't believe it.'

After twenty days in hospital I was given the all clear to return to the UK. The doctors and nurses who had kept me alive and looked after me so well gave me an emotional fare-well, and even as I was being wheeled down the corridor, nurses kissed my cheek and posed for photographs. Having my life saved multiple times was humbling and almost em-barrassing. It's difficult to know what to say as you can never repay them, and words can't express true sentiments at even a fraction of their real worth.

My parents travelled in the back of the ambulance with me on the way to Bucharest airport. The journey was tense: one of the airline's conditions of carriage was to have a nurse accompany us to the UK, but my mother, long since retired from the profession had negotiated her way into the role. The hospital had signed the relevant papers and we just hoped the airline wouldn't be too thorough in their checks. Upon boarding my dad realized that we hadn't been given my pass-port by the officials handling my immunity from security and immigration. We kept quiet and hoped nobody would notice, but they did. The doors were reopened and a panic-stricken official climbed on board waving my passport in his hand. We were so traumatized from everything that had happened, we genuinely feared we'd be asked to get off the plane and lose our seats. For the three of us we were required to have six seats, four of which were for a special stretcher that could be fitted onto the top of the seat heads. The four-hour flight was a stressful time. In spite of my mother's nursing experience we all knew that if I experienced another relapse I would be done for.

At Heathrow airport I was stretchered off the plane by medics and taken through back doors to bypass the usual entry checks. Surprisingly, there were a few journalists waiting around for a story. The airport doctor briefed my parents and instructed the driver to take me to a London hospital. I wanted to be near to my family and London was a long drive from Shropshire, so my dad hired a car, folded the back seats down, padded it out with pillows and sleeping bags and drove me to the hospital in my home town. We arrived late and being admitted was full of drama as my parents had to go through the rigmarole of explaining my condition, my unannounced arrival, and why I had not stayed in a London hospital as instructed. I was kept waiting in the back of the car for over an hour before a stretcher eventually came for me.

It was a Saturday morning and my first day in Shrewsbury hospital. I had woken early to find my parents had gone and the ward dead quiet and depressingly inactive. Alone, bored and anxious for news, there was nothing to do apart from wait for my brother Mick to arrive. Doctors' rounds started an hour later on weekends and it wasn't until 9 o'clock that a doctor reached me. He was direct and abrupt in his analysis: my hip was irreparable and it was unlikely I would walk again. Heartbroken, I kept questioning him, searching for a glimmer of hope. His replies were professional, but they sounded cold and I was left feeling as though I was wasting his time. He advised me to transfer to somewhere with more orthopaedic expertise and recommended Stoke. After he'd gone, I lay stunned. I'd already heard it before in Romania, but delivered by a British doctor in my home-town hospital, the words seemed to acquire a more potent meaning. At first I was filled with a rage I couldn't express, but exhaustion prevented reaction. Then I looked down at my legs, struggling to accept that some guy was telling me it was over. No more army, climbing or football. I don't think the doctor understood what he was saying to me or who he was saying it to. He didn't know that being physically active was my entire life. I fumbled around not knowing what to do with myself and tightened my eyes so I didn't cry. Even though I was lying down my knees trembled and I dissolved in tears.

After several miserable days in Shrewsbury hospital, I moved to Stoke under the joint care of an orthopaedic surgeon and a gastric specialist. I was placed on an orthopaedic ward, even though it was my stomach that required the more urgent and day-to-day treatment. On my first meeting with a consultant it was reiterated to me that the chances of a return to an active lifestyle were improbable. The best I could hope for was a full hip replacement, which would allow me to lead a normal but physically inactive life. The more likely alternative was to have my hip fused, which meant the joint would be permanently fixed, reducing my movement to a severe limp and a walking stick for the rest of my life.

The next two months were a long and painful period of surgery and recovery. The four drainage tubes were still connected to my stomach, my leg was back in traction and a course of drugs with unpleasant side effects combined to make life uncomfortable. My early intentions of staying positive slowly fell by the wayside and most of my energy was sapped as I spent more and more time dwelling on my future. After a few weeks, the laziness of recovery had set in and I started to become a product of my environment. I was surrounded by sick people, and some of them seemed to enjoy it, if only for the attention they received and the camaraderie of collective injury or ill health they shared with other patients. I started to believe I was sick because everything around me told me I was. All my basic needs were catered for, and being so weak, I became totally dependent on others. I was like a grown-up child, the nurses carried out every task for me:

washing me and even changing the nappies I had to wear because of my stomach condition. Almost without noticing, I had entered into a passive state and turned into a grumpy, short-fused, bitter and unhappy person. I became an increasing burden to my family, venting anger or frustration on the people who deserved it least. I found myself cursing them over the most trivial things. Even bringing the wrong flavour breakfast cereal or arriving minutes late was enough to set me off.

I quickly started to resent being in hospital and much of my bitterness was compounded by and directed at other patients. I somehow convinced myself I was a special case, and the monotony of my daily routine didn't help my state of mind. Between visits I watched TV, ate whatever I could get my hands on and read crappy magazines and tabloid newspapers. The start and end of each day was dominated by the twice daily shots to reduce my stomach acid levels. The drugs had awful side effects and for the thirty dreaded minutes that followed my mind would cloud over in a nightmare level of consciousness where everything took on a grey and lumpy feel. It wasn't even pain, more of a dreariness where light hurt my eyes and I could no longer talk in sentences. Needing to be alone and undisturbed, I hid beneath the sheets and would not come out until the effects wore off.

After five weeks in Stoke I'd more or less given up all hope and was resigned to an uncertain and inactive future. It took an incident with a nurse to snap me out of my stupor and revive something of the positive fighting spirit that I'd always had before. At the end of another day at odds with the care staff and nurses, one took it upon herself to give me a piece of her mind. She sat at the side of my bed and asked me if I would like to see a psychologist. Before waiting for my answer, she added that in her professional opinion, I needed psychological help. For a few seconds I was stunned into silence, thinking she must have got the wrong patient.

'I don't want or need to speak with anyone,' I said, 'and I'll deal with my problems in my own way.'

'You know what your problem is? You need to learn to accept that you are sick. You're in hospital and the advice of the doctors and nurses is best for you. You also need to accept that you won't be able to walk again,' she snapped back at me.

I dismissed her with a volley of angry remarks, adding that I never wanted to see her at my bed again. I hit the buzzer and requested the pay phone on wheels. I called home and asked someone to visit as soon as possible.

A few hours alone were enough to bring about a drastic turnaround in my outlook. I was now more determined than ever to stay positive and put all my efforts into recovering as quickly as possible. I would deal with my leg when I had my general health back. From then on I refused to see myself as a sick man any longer and, starting the next morning, I began a policy of non-cooperation. I insisted the curtains remained closed around my bed throughout the day so that I didn't see the constant stream of nurses and sick people coming in and out. I wouldn't allow the care workers to clean me and instead requested warm water and fresh towels so I could do it myself. I refused the pain killers which I'd become dependent on and became deaf to anything a doctor might say on their rounds each morning. With this self-sufficiency my morale improved and my stress disappeared. The only people I paid any attention to were my gastric surgeon, Professor Elder, and the ward sister, everyone else was ignored. I was embarking on my own programme of recovery; I would get better and do it my way. Time was precious and I was impatient, I could no longer afford to listen to the textbook rhetorical advice of the doctors and nurses. Each time I did, they sowed fresh seeds of doubt in my mind.

A week into my new recovery plan a hurried nurse mistakenly left my personal medical file on the bedside cabinet. Naturally I read it: I was a troublesome patient, with discipline problems and an attitude of intolerance to hospital staff. They did not reflect my view as a patient: that the hospital was understaffed and that the ward was heavily reliant on undertrained agency care workers, some of whom were lazy and unprofessional. I asked a visitor to take the file with him and throw it away, it was a petty act, but at the time it felt satisfying. No doubt another more damning report would be written up, but I was beyond caring. Not long after this incident I was removed from orthopaedics into my own private room on the gastric ward. The patients on ward nine cheered as I was wheeled away, one even shouted out 'good riddance' as the doors closed behind me. I took it as a compliment: I wasn't one of them and wouldn't join their club.

The shift sister personally welcomed me onto ward sixteen.

'I've heard all about you,' she said with a smile on her face, 'and I don't believe a word of it. You're going to be well looked after here and you should specifically ask for me if you have any problems.'

Later she told me that orthopaedics had not been the right place for me to get the care I needed. She was surprised I had been sent there considering how far away my hip was from being treatable, and that I needed to be in a specialist ward able to provide the care and know-how to deal with a gastric problem as severe as mine. With this change hospital life became immediately more bearable, and for the remainder of my time in Stoke I kept the same rotation of pleasant and professional nurses and had trouble-free interactions with all the medical staff. Having a private room allowed me to receive a constant stream of visits from family and friends from the army and university. It was invigorating to be sociable again, simply being able to have conversations about normal things gave me renewed verve as well as something to look forward to each day. Two friends from my university halls gave me highly entertaining visits and were subsequently warned by my mother not to make me laugh as the contractions were pulling at my stitches.

The most emotionally charged visit came on the day of a consultation with an experienced orthopaedic surgeon I hadn't seen before. Three close friends from my former army unit made the journey up from London bringing a crate of Guinness with them, and in no time, they had made themselves comfortable and were cracking open cans and in full storytelling mode. They soon had me recounting my escape from the mountain, which from start to finish took up most of the afternoon. The surgeon arrived at four o'clock sharp. I was nervous but eager to learn if he had anything promising to say, and when he suggested that I might like to ask my friends to leave the room, I said there were no secrets between us and they could stay as I needed their support. Without wasting a moment he told me the X-rays showed only slight signs of improvement to the hip and the damage was so extensive that there was little in the way of solid structure to work with. My prospects for an active working hip were slim, but with time and luck, I would be able to have the joint fused. After these words I couldn't concentrate on anything else he said. I had asked that my friends stayed and now felt ashamed to have received this diagnosis in front of them. It was as though my not being able to walk again had somehow let them down. The very basis of our friendship and everything we had done together was built around physical activity, and now I could no longer be part of it.

After the consultant left, I fought to hold back my tears and avoided my friends' eyes. My lower lip was wobbling uncontrollably and I couldn't find a dignified way to respond. My friend Justin issued an inspirational rallying call, hitting me with a response true to his character and style.

'Don't you dare listen to them, mate. They don't know anything about you, who you are, what you've done or what you're capable of. You will walk again, Ken, I know you will and so do you. There is no way in hell it isn't going to happen. You just gotta be patient and you will be back to your former glory. Fuck 'em, mate.'

By the time he was finished I couldn't fight back the tears.

The final three weeks were a relatively easy time, the biggest battle was fighting the boredom and maintaining self-belief and motivation. Fortunately the bedside chair was nearly always occupied by a member of my family or a friend, so I rarely had the time or opportunity to feel lonely or down.

In these difficult times their love and friendship was every bit as valuable to my recovery as the medical attention I received. It was also interesting to see who visited; some people who I never thought would had surprised me, and others who I regarded as good friends never came. The highlight of each week and the only event that differentiated one day from the next was being able to watch *Match of the Day* on Saturday nights with my brother Mick and a hamper of goodies. I knew I should have been using the time to read great books, or to do some of my own writing, but I was still feeling sorry for myself and simply lacked the motivation and drive to engage in anything worthwhile.

As my condition improved, I began to see more of both surgeons dealing with my stomach and hip. The man in charge of my stomach, Professor Elder, had carried out some amazing work in getting me functioning again and was always willing and able to explain my condition in the simplest way. He was an inspiration, although he claimed to be nothing more than a simple plumber. By the eighth week the drains were removed from my stomach and I was stitched up. I felt liberated to be free of pipes and drips, my range of movement increased tenfold and I rediscovered many basic things I hadn't been able to do in a long time. Being able to shower made me feel truly clean for the first time in ages, and rejuvenated my energy levels. Going outside for fresh air improved my morale and outlook. The ability to sit up in bed also made me more attentive to my guests and increased my concentration span and ability to focus. The big difference was being able to roll onto my front. I slept like a log and experienced my most deep and uninterrupted sleep in four months.

Towards the end of my time in Stoke, my case began to attract the interest of a number of orthopaedic surgeons throughout the country. Injuries like mine were infrequent and provided an exciting opportunity for any experienced surgeon to work with strong young bones. At first all the attention was flattering, but I soon felt like a case study or experiment as I grew to realize it was my hip and not me as a person they cared about. I lost count of how many I saw, only distinguishing between those who were more encouraging than others. There was talk of me going to Oswestry, a famous orthopaedic centre just outside my home county, but in the end I was advised to remain in Stoke under the care of a doctor there who was regarded as one of the country's foremost surgeons in his field.

After three months the treatment on my stomach came to an end and I was functioning on a normal level. The condition of my hip was less straightforward and was still too complicated to operate on. However, the X-rays revealed that the bone was solidifying at an improved rate and it was recommended that I waited at least eight months to see what the hip did, by which time there might be enough solid bone to drill into. As for my frostbite, there was no hard and fast treatment, the skin on the underside of my foot was still hard and black, it always hurt a lot and I'd lost the ends of four toes. They had gradually decayed from cell death and lack of oxygen due to constricted blood flow to my extremities. The Romanians had told me it would take at least a year to regain some feeling, in which time my toes might fall off anyway. I could either have them amputated or wait, so I decided to wait. I signed my release papers and checked out of hospital with instructions to take plenty of rest and eat as much as I could, with only a third of a stomach remaining it would be impossible to get fat. After four months incapacitated in a hospital bed I was overjoyed to be going home. I phoned my little brother and told him the news, it was the happiest I had felt since I was under my snow shelter drinking hot chocolate on the slopes of the Fagaras.

CHAPTER FOURTEEN

BACK HOME

The next six months were spent in the countryside at the family home in Shropshire. I slept downstairs in the lounge on a specially adapted high bed, the toilet had a raised seat connected to a frame on wheels and the televisions were swapped around so I could use the one with the remote control. My crutches and a urine container hung from the side of my bed and an easily reachable shelf was fixed to the wall to hold books, water and everything else I needed to get through the day. I was still more or less a patient, but gone were the little daily reminders that I was a sick person: blood tests, injections, doctors' rounds and the unnerving bleep of electronic monitoring equipment.

I slipped happily into a routine that remained unchanged for a couple of weeks. I woke early, watched the morning news and waited for someone to help me get dressed. The order was always the same, one sock went on first as my frostbitten foot was left to air and then my legs fed into some loose-fitting tracksuit trousers, which I managed pull up myself. To put a T-shirt on I had to be lifted upright, as I still hadn't developed the stomach muscles to sit myself up. After lying horizontal for so many months, it was important I spent time out of the bed to restore my body's equilibrium and also to prevent bed sores. I was still so weak and unstable that my first attempt to stand caused me to faint, but luckily my brother was quick enough to catch my fall. Subsequent attempts still left me light headed and my knees were susceptible to buckling beneath my weight. Bathing was always a difficult procedure and impossible to do without assistance, the task being all the more challenging due to my frostbitten foot, which still had to be kept dry to avoid the possibility of gangrene. This normally involved wrapping three or four plastic bags around my foot and taping them at the ankle, but even after such measures I kept the leg elevated so that it could hang over the side of the bath while I washed. One of my brothers was always there in case I suffered one of my dizzy spells and drowned. For those early weeks I had to be closely guarded.

As I gained strength I soon learnt that for every action I wanted to carry out, I was quickly able to develop an adaptation to compensate for my disabilities. It amazed me how my body could find its way around any problem. All it needed was patience and imagination to find alternatives that worked nearly as well. Getting out of bed unassisted proved the most testing of my early challenges. With the foot of my good leg, I would gently push the injured one across the bed until it was positioned at the edge of the mattress. Then, hooking the toes of the good leg under the ankle of the useless one, I could gently lower both legs so that they hung off the bed. With assistance from the wall, I could sit upright and get into position to lower myself to the ground. Before moving off, I cautiously distributed my weight between crutches and the good leg, and made sure my arms were up to holding the strain.

After the rigmarole of leaving my bed each morning, I always took a little stroll around the house, at first no further than the kitchen as I was still prone to dizzy spells and too weak to cover much distance. Although I relied entirely upon my crutches, those few steps each day felt like massive strides on my road to recovery. Within a matter of weeks, I'd managed to venture outside onto the patio; it was only 30 metres from my bed but arriving there left me shattered and out of breath. My upper-body muscles had wasted so badly that they were hardly able to take my weight through the crutches and making it back always took it out of me. I'd get back into bed exhausted and sleep for another hour before waking again at nine for breakfast: the same every day, porridge followed by a full English fry up. The rest of my meals weren't much healthier, but since I was still about 28 kilos under weight, doctor's orders overrode any sensible diet plan. The rest of the day I would be left in bed while my family went about their business.

Throughout this period my prospects for recovery, and what I'd be able to do and not do, constantly played on my mind. At this time many of my military friends were deployed on lucrative security contracts in the Middle East and others had exciting jobs with the army and navy. I knew that my soldiering career was probably over, but the hardest part was accepting that I was no longer physically able to do what I'd done for so long. Dropping out of university was every bit as demoralizing – it had been hard work getting there and I'd thoroughly enjoyed the experience. The overriding feeling was one of being left behind and thoughts of adjusting to a new way of life revolted and scared me. I didn't want to adapt or change who I was, I wanted to be the old me again. My attitude was symptomatic of having so much time on my hands and so little to do.

As summer approached I began to spend more of each day outside. My mother kept a beautiful garden full of brightly coloured flowers in neat rows, with an old water well with a red-tiled roof and a long arched walkway covered in ivy and creeping plants. A menagerie of animals – peacocks, guinea fowl, ducks, chickens, geese and goats – roamed the grounds. I was lucky to have the perfect place to recover and being outdoors reignited my enthusiasm and levels of optimism. My morale quickly started to pick up and I began to use everything I was missing out on as motivation to get better. Beyond the gardens was an open stretch of moorland and a range of rolling hills; I'd often find myself staring out across them and imagining what lay on the other side, almost as though I'd forgotten or only seen it in a dream. Before I had joined the army I'd stared across the hills in the same way, wide-eyed and excited by infinite possibilities at what the wider world might hold for me.

Although it was well into spring, looking out of my window one afternoon at a late flurry of snowfall, I was reminded of one of my earliest memories from when I was four years old.

One morning I sneaked into my mother's room, trying not to wake her as she had just worked a night shift at the hospital. Inside her wardrobe was a pair of unworn men's working boots that fascinated me. Each time I pulled them out my mother would tell me they were mine as soon as I was big enough to fit them. I looked out of the window and saw snow for the first time that I remember; it was already deep and still falling heavily. I was enthralled that the world could look so different and found myself staring down the road, the end of which was no longer visible through the blur of thick snowfall. Entranced, I couldn't take my eyes away, imagining it leading into some far-off fantastic and magical land. I was hit by a powerful urge to be outside, exploring and seeing the world beyond my street. My heart had started beating faster at the prospect, provoking me to open the cupboard and quietly search out the boots. When I found them, I examined every part at every angle, obsessed by the thick laces and enormous rubber grips on the soles. I'd grown a shoe size when I was recently measured and though the boots were still too big, I tried them on, tied the laces as tight as I could manage and shuffled back over to the window. I stared out longingly, wanting to make that step into the unknown, beyond the street to a place I'd never been alone. Yet for all my ambitions and curiosity, I was too scared to leave my mum.

It was a powerful memory and perhaps explained why I had always been so fascinated by snow and winter. I wondered how I would have felt if I had stepped out into the snow on my own and gone beyond the bottom of the street which I had never walked without my mother. Within this recollection I detected a message; if I wanted to get beyond those hills again and see the world, all I had to do was find the courage to walk. It was as if some sort of mental block had been lifted, and inspired by possibility, I heaved myself up onto my crutches and started walking. I headed straight down the garden path beneath the ivy archway, cautiously positioning my crutches on the loose, snow-covered chippings. At the end of the path there were three steps leading up onto the road. Putting all my weight through my good leg, I positioned my crutches onto the middle step and pole-vaulted up to the top. This was already double as far as I'd gone before and, about to go further still, I heard my mother call, 'Oh my God, where's Kenneth?' My little brother Craig ran outside and began looking around for me, then started laughing when he saw me.

'He's up on the road,' he called back.

He ran down the pathway and asked me, 'How the hell did you get up the steps?'

To demonstrate my new-found agility I cleared all three steps down onto the path in a single hop. Nobody in my family could believe I was moving about so freely. For close to six months I had been confined to my bed, and after weeks at home, I had ventured no further than the patio. State of mind had played such a strong part between what I was willing and able to do. Feeling some fight back in me, I hopped back to my bed and slept until mid-afternoon. Those few small steps initiated my body's return to a level of active function, and the next day I was back on the garden path and up onto the road. A few days later I'd reached the barn in the paddock and within the week, I was crossing fields and had started to feed the chickens. As my strength returned progressively, I went out two or three times a day.

Life at home changed for the better for me and my family. I became more independent and sought to do everything except cooking for myself. Each day I would go for long walks alone, and on the days I felt strong, I would cover up to three miles on a return journey. My frostbitten foot was mostly left to heal uncovered, except when I walked. On these occasions it would be heavily bandaged and strapped into a size thirteen open-toed sandal. Every so often I would visit my GP or attend an outpatients' clinic to have my frostbite examined, and it soon became a star attraction with the medical staff, some travelling from afar to get eyes on an actual case.

Similarly, most of my guests would want to look at my foot when they visited, some liked to tap it with their fingers or bang it with a metal spoon. As my strength grew and I gained weight, my doctors and physiotherapists decided it was important for me to start swimming a couple of times a week in order to counter the effects of severe muscle atrophy. I was eager to get going again, but didn't want to go against the advice of the Romanians and get my foot wet. It was still black and painful underneath, but slowly bits of the thick, dead, black skin were falling away, leaving me with a delicate layer of soft, highly sensitive, new pink skin beneath.

Throughout the five months I spent at home, I had frequent consultations with my orthopaedic surgeon. By late July little had changed and he told me that my two options remained the same: the joint could be fused or I could wait and hope that I might be able to receive a full hip replacement. Although neither appealed to me, the latter seemed my only hope, the mere suggestion of a fused joint enraged me more and more each time he said it. The only encouraging news came from the X-rays, which showed that the bone in my hip was solidifying, albeit slowly.

Armed with the knowledge that my bones were gradually repairing, I started to research hip replacements, what the operation involved and what it would allow the recipient to do in terms of an active lifestyle. There seemed to be surprisingly little information on, or case examples of, recipients around my age group or activity level. The cited cases were mostly elderly or severely overweight people who generally had little need or desire to be physically active. I discovered that some athletes had had procedures similar to the one I might be looking at, but none had ever returned to a competitive level. A hip replacement at least gave me hope that I might walk again, and that was enough to keep me going.

CHAPTER FIFTEEN

ALL THINGS MUST PASS

By late August I had been home as long as I'd been in hospital, and I lacked any sort of constructive goals other than to walk again. It was the first time in my adult life that I had nothing concrete to work towards. Sitting in bed, watching crap on TV, occasional outings to the supermarket and walking to my village and back on crutches were no longer enough. On the morning of the first of September, nine months after my accident, I made the decision to return to university. The afternoon of the same day I informed the history department and started an accommodation search. As the ball got rolling I felt a nervous energy at the prospect of leaving the sanctuary of home life. I knew it was going to be a challenge, but felt ready to start again. What I looked forward to most was telling my friends I was coming back.

The first week after my return passed comfortably and I soon got back into the flow of studying and actually started to enjoy using my brain again. Managing to attend all of my lectures and tutorials felt like a significant achievement, and unexpectedly, I found that I loved the routine of a work schedule as it gave me a strong sense of purpose and took my mind away from many of my physical problems. Within a month I had established a good routine of studying and began to gain a little more confidence in myself and my ability to manoeuvre between home and campus. Occasionally, I suffered unexpected dizzy spells, which would sometimes hit me in a lecture theatre, causing me to fall asleep, but I felt sure I wasn't the first student to do that. Most weeks there would be a day when I lacked the strength to make it into lectures, but there was always someone who would lend me their notes.

While I was coping with the academic workload, my return to university was far from plain sailing. I hadn't anticipated many of the extra challenges that came with being a disabled student. Simply carrying out basic chores, such as cooking and shopping turned into draining activities. My heavy dependence on close friends wasn't lost on me, and I was aware that without them my return wouldn't have been possible. There was a multitude of other tasks that proved difficult to negotiate: climbing and descending staircases in the older department buildings, fitting into narrow toilet cubicles, the need for an outside seat in lecture theatres to stretch out my injured leg and the essential task of locating and borrowing books from the university library. Even bus travel was a tricky proposition on one leg. After boarding it was typical of the driver to start off again before I had sat down, and if I wasn't quick getting off, I would miss my stop unless I shouted. The worst part was getting a seat, the buses were often crammed and it was hit and miss that someone would give up their place. I hadn't given these things a moment's thought in my first year, but they were now daily challenges. As I learnt and adjusted to my own limits, I became correspondingly aware of other people in a similar position to myself. Whereas before I had hardly ever noticed, now I started to see disability all around me. I began paying close attention to how they coped with everyday tasks and obstacles, watching whether they were competent, struggling or disguising their difficulties. I also put special emphasis into concentrating on their faces, trying to gauge if they were happy or not. They all looked purposeful; now I understood they had to be.

As the first semester neared its end, I dedicated increasing amounts of time into researching hip replacements and alternative treatments. The McMinn, a relatively new procedure, looked promising. It involved resurfacing the joints with a metal ball and socket, rather than completely replacing the femoral head with an artificial joint. Not only would a resurfacing job allow its recipients to be active, it would still give the option of a full hip replacement further down the line. At my next consultation the X-rays showed increasing signs of repair, satisfying my doctor enough to give me a provisional date for a hip replacement. After over a year of not being able to walk without crutches this was the best news I could have received.

A few weeks after the post-Christmas examinations, I received two pieces of unwelcome mail on the same day. The first one was from Stoke hospital informing me that my operation date had been put back an additional three months due to a reshuffling of the waiting list. The other letter was from the Disability Department of my local social services, notifying me that I was entitled to a four-wheel motorized invalid buggy. A brochure was enclosed so that I could choose the model that best suited my needs. It was a real kick in the teeth. I'd come to think of myself as somebody with an injury who occasionally used disabled facilities. Now I realized that other people had a completely different way of classifying me. I felt a mixture of fury and sadness at the postponement and thoughts of a motorized vehicle, but when I showed the letter to my friend and student flatmate Pete expecting some sympathy, he pointed out that I was entitled to two buggies and joked that we could ride into campus together and go supermarket shopping. It was hard not to laugh, having Pete around had an immeasurable effect on my morale. I wallowed in self-pity for a few hours before the sadness morphed into fury, and from that point on I decided to walk absolutely everywhere. That evening, I left the apartment as usual and instead of catching the bus, I set off on an anger-fuelled walk, covering the five miles to the student village and back on my crutches in no time at all. The exertion made me realize I had far more strength than I had previously thought. The next day I fitted a pull-up bar in the living room doorway and conceived of a rule where each time Pete or I walked under the bar we owed it ten pull-ups. I let my friends know I intended to start some hard training, hoping that they would join me.

Two days later, as I stood outside Openshaw Youth Centre waiting for friends, I was hit by early waves of anxiety about what I was letting myself in for. It was a typically cold, rainy and dark Manchester evening which seemed to concentrate my thoughts towards the impending suffering. As I made my way down the narrow basement staircase to Shannon's gym, I was immediately hit by the smell of sweat and could make out the rhythmic snap of skipping ropes whipping down onto the wooden floor against the beat of hard rap music. Inside, it felt as though I was stepping back in time: the same tunes boomed from the stereo, the same old tough-guy faces whacking the punch bags and the same stink. As I made my way across the gym on my crutches a few old faces looked up and gave us a nod, others gave us the 'what are these students doing here?' stares that I'd seen a hundred times before. My fear of this place was quick to return, it was the House of Pain as Bob liked to call it. Now I was back for more.

Bob Shannon managed the gym and was also the head trainer. His reputation was for his conditioning work and I'd heard about him through military circles long before I ever met him. The words, 'He could pass Selection now, even at forty-two,' remained firmly in my mind. I found him in the Ring Room. It was a matter of courtesy to let him know I was back and request permission to train in his gym. I stood leaning on my crutches while he shouted instructions at the two fighters in the ring then, when the bell rang, I stepped up and jokingly introduced myself as if we had never met before. Bob invited me into his office where we talked about a training programme tailored to my capabilities. He never once discouraged me and only talked about the positives of being active again. I gave him the low-down on my medical condition, but he just shrugged his shoulders when I told him.

'That's no problem, Kenny, you'll be back in shape in no time.'

Bob stopped me just as I was leaving the office for the changing room and presented me with a Shannon's Gym 'Fighting Fit' T-shirt and congratulated me for making it off the mountain alive.

'Not many people would have made it back from that, Kenny,' he said.

Coming from a man like Bob, I valued such words as high praise.

Out on the training floor I placed my crutches up against the wall and grabbed the longest leather skipping rope I could find. Standing on one leg in a clear space, I tried to skip, but the rope caught my foot on the first revolution. After trying several times with no success, Bob's wife suggested I pushed my bad leg tight against my good one. On the next attempt I managed close to ten. I kept working at it and within half an hour the leather rope became a blur as I maintained a fast rhythm for over a minute at a time. I hadn't been this out of breath for fourteen months and it felt good. I also managed some press-ups and a few sessions of having a heavy medicine ball smashed into my stomach.

Bob insisted I finish with a workout on the bags.

'This one's for you, Kenny,' he shouted across the gym as he turned up the stereo to the opening riff of 'Eye of the Tiger'.

I started hitting the bag as hard as it was possible for someone balancing on one leg. At the end of the session I didn't even have the energy to shower, and it was as much as I could manage to climb the stairs out of the gym. When the blast of cold air hit me outside, my leg nearly gave way and seconds later I collapsed onto the pavement from exhaustion. My friends had to lift me into the car and carry me back to my apartment, but I was back at Bob's the next evening.

The next few months were a blur of training and studying. I attended Shannon's Gym at least three times a week and maintained my regime with the pull-up bar when at home. Most evenings after visiting friends I sat behind my laptop in Owens Park computer centre, working until the early hours researching hip replacements and writing essays. Every day I walked at least five miles and I'd become a regular face at Manchester Royal Infirmary Physiotherapy Department as a result. I was putting in so many miles that the rubber crutch tips required fortnightly replacements.

While I was busy I was fairly content; there was rarely time for me to dwell on my condition or be depressed. I was eating well and steadily regained some of the muscle I had lost in hospital. My health was improving, university was great and my prospect for a strong recovery looked ever more likely. I was hit with some more bad news in March when I was informed that my operation had been put back for a second time. Initially I was angry and upset, but quickly saw the postponement could work to my advantage. Firstly, it gave me more time to research alternative procedures and also meant that I wouldn't have to miss the final semester and have to take re-sit examinations the following year.

Just as I was starting to map out my future an event took place that turned my plans upside down. It was a Wednesday evening, Manchester United were drawn to play at home against Bayer Leverkusen in the Champions League football competition. I usually watched the games on TV at home, but that night I'd taken my friend Alex out to dinner as a way of saying thank you for his support. As we were about to take the bus home a man with a German accent approached us, he and his friends had been to the match and were looking for a good restaurant. After I recommended a place he asked me what had happened to my leg. I gave him a brief but polite answer, which I was by now well versed in doing. Looking concerned he pointed out his two friends waiting on the other side of the road.

'My friend over there is one of Germany's best hip surgeons,' he told us.

He then called over the two men, both wearing Bayer Leverkusen scarves. They shook hands with us and politely introduced themselves. My first impression was that they'd had a few beers. The hip surgeon, Dr Jontschew, then asked me to tell him what had happened to my leg and even though I was unsure if this was just drunken banter, I told him nonetheless. He absorbed the facts and enquired about my surgeon along with the possibility of a resurfacing (McMinn) procedure. I explained to him that my surgeon was highly experienced and had said it couldn't be done. He paused for a moment and said something along the lines of, 'Yes, but the

Germans, they are the best . . . and the Swiss are very good too,' probably adding the latter not to sound biased towards his countrymen.

I laughed and said that I didn't doubt it, but he looked at me with a stern expression on his face.

'I am not joking. You cannot have a hip replacement,' he said. 'You are too young. It will be the end for you.'

My heart sank as he hit me with the hard truth that I'd long known but had pushed to the back of my mind. I asked for his contact details and wrote his email address down on a piece of scrap paper. He warned me that he would have to see my X-rays to know if the McMinn procedure was possible and the sooner the better.

I was unable to sleep that night as my mind buzzed with the good fortune of my encounter and the possibility that I might be able to have the McMinn procedure after all.

Although the NHS were reluctant to release my scans, a bit of skulduggery ensured we got our hands on them. On the day that my brother Mick flew to Munich with them, I sat restlessly behind a computer screen in Owens Park. My brother was making a journey that could alter the course of my life, but all I could do was wait and anticipate a phone call or email. I stayed up until the early hours of the next day, but on hearing nothing I took the long walk home and slept for a few hours. It wasn't until late afternoon that I received an email from Mick requesting that I call his mobile. With butterflies in my stomach, I hopped like a madman to a phone box and made the call.

'OK, listen carefully,' he said. 'Don't get too excited but Jontschew said the McMinn could be done.'

'That's amazing,' I said as if it were good news for someone else.

I didn't know what else to say apart from offering my repeated thanks. Mick continued, telling me that because of my injuries the operation would still be very difficult, but the longer I waited, the better my chances. He flew back into Manchester the next morning and I skipped lectures and spent the rest of the day talking over everything he had learned in Germany. Until this time I hadn't considered the practicalities or logistics of the operation, I'd only concerned myself with whether it was possible or not. Dr Jontschew had offered to perform the surgery, but it was likely to be an expensive affair with the addition of flights to Germany and follow-up appointments. Most importantly I had to be convinced of making the right choice before cancelling my hip replacement with the NHS.

Over the next few days I communicated with Dr Jontschew via email and telephone. He understood the burden and costs of surgery out of country and suggested there would be someone in the UK who would be able to carry out the operation as well as he could, even if it wasn't Mr McMinn himself. He also said that looking for a surgeon or any health care was like shopping. 'You have to look round and assess all the options before making a choice.' He advised me it was unwise to accept the medical opinion of only one person and that I should carry out my own research to find out who was most capable and experienced. I was also warned that any surgeon would jump at the chance to carry out a standard hip replacement on me given that such opportunities to test their skills on young people or athletes were so uncommon. I appreciated this honesty and saw that Jontschew was a man of integrity who had nothing but my best interests in mind.

I now had two weeks to consider my course of action before having blood tests and one final consultation at Stoke. If I didn't find a surgeon who could carry out the McMinn before that time, I was obliged to give my doctor at Stoke a firm decision so that he could order the parts and acquire the donor bone from a bone bank. If I called the operation off and got it wrong, I would be pushed to the bottom of the waiting list at the NHS.

On a Friday afternoon during the Easter break my series of lucky encounters took another twist. I received a phone call from my mother, flustered and excited, asking me to come home immediately before even explaining why. Only moments before she had received a visit from Mick Boulton, the owner of a fleet of buses headquartered in my home village of Cardington. He had occasionally driven me to school when I was a young boy, but I best remembered him as a serious runner and a pretty tough guy. It was common knowledge in the small community that Mick had suffered a serious injury to his hip while cycling in France. My mum went on to explain that he had received the same resurfacing operation that I was desperate to have, so I made my way directly to Piccadilly station and caught the train back home.

I sat idle for a few days and filled up on home cooking until Mick was free to visit. I was a little apprehensive at the prospect of his arrival as my main memories of him were watching him go on crazy long runs into the mountains; and incurring his wrath as a teenager after causing trouble on his bus. I was half hoping he wouldn't remember me but he did, and he cracked a few jokes about various incidents. After a brief chat I gave him a full account of my injuries followed by my situation. Mick also shared his experience, detailing the procedure, his surgeon and his post-operation physical capabilities. Everything he said pleased me and the evidence of it was right there in front of me; Mick was in brilliant physical condition, running occasionally and training solidly on his road bike. I had always known he was a fit guy, but to hear what he was doing in his fifties, post hip surgery, was astonishing. His story was inspirational and convinced me that I had to have a McMinn at all costs. The day reached its climax when Mick said he would contact his surgeon, Mr Isbister, and offered to go with me to see him at his practice in Wolverhampton. Mick's advice and encouragement was all I needed to help me reach a final decision.

With the date for my hip replacement at Stoke less than a month away I had to inform the hospital of my intention to cancel the operation. The dilemma I faced was that I still didn't know if the McMinn could be done, making any decision a gamble. My mum and brother accompanied me to Stoke for my final pre-op consultation. It wasn't until we were in the waiting room that I broke the news to my mother that I was definitely going to cancel the operation. As I walked out the hospital and across the car park I felt a huge weight had been lifted from my shoulders, almost as though I had been liberated from an imminent doom and was free once more.

A couple of weeks later I had my first appointment with Mr Isbister. As promised, Mick Boulton drove me and my mother to Wolverhampton and offered to accompany us for the consultation. I was glad to have him there as the anticipation of medical verdicts often overwhelmed me. Sometimes I almost didn't want to know as the uncertainty was often preferable to the possibility of bad news. But in spite of my apprehension Mr Isbister came across as a serious and optimistic man with a determination to tackle tough procedures, so I liked what he said and had confidence in him immediately. After taking his own X-rays he delivered the verdict I had been so anxiously waiting for, he could do the McMinn resurfacing procedure. At a follow-up appointment ten days later, I was given a choice of dates for the operation. Considering how long I had already waited and the health benefits of delay, I opted for a later date so that I could stay at university and sit the end of year exams which would count towards my final degree. For the first time since my accident I could feel my ordeal drawing to a close; it was the most certain and happiest I had felt in a long time.

CHAPTER SIXTEEN

POST OP

The first words Mr Isbister said to me when I came round from the operation was that it had been one of the hardest jobs he had ever done. He quickly followed up on his remark by telling me the operation had been a success. Even under the carefree and hazy effects of anaesthesia I felt a huge wave of relief, happiness and peace. I managed to say thank you and held out my hand to shake his. Within minutes I was asleep again.

I passed the summer months recovering from the operation at my parents' new home in the Welsh countryside. Complete success wouldn't be determined until my next consultation which was eight weeks down the road. If my bone had accepted the donor bone, and the metal pins and joints were still in place with no sign of infection, I would be off my crutches as soon as the X-rays came up. I tried not to dwell on what was now out of both mine and Mr Isbister's hands, instead I fostered the belief that I had been through too much for it all to come undone at the last hurdle. Somehow I just knew I was going to be alright.

With my siblings in different parts of the world, I spent much of each day on the sofa in front of the TV. For three weeks I was entertained by the European football championships and the remainder of the time I took long walks in the sun and daydreamed of countries I wanted to visit and mountains I wanted to climb. As my important date drew closer I began to think with greater confidence about what new physical activity I might pursue with two working legs. I wanted to be active again and was desperate for a challenge to make up for everything I felt I had missed out on over the last two years. One evening I sat watching the TV highlights of a Tour de France stage, and was impressed by the commentator proclaiming the race as the world's most physically demanding sporting event. I watched with a keen eye and felt the early waves of interest and motivation run through me. The next day I bought a copy of Tim Krabbe's *The Rider* and developed an enthusiasm for cycling even though I'd never really ridden before. Inspired, I found myself thinking about bikes and training regimes during my daily walks. It got me excited and helped relieve the boredom that had been ever present since coming away from Manchester.

The day of my final consultation came quite unemotionally. I was accompanied by my mum and my youngest brother, Craig. The X-rays came up digitally on a computer screen, and after a careful study Mr Isbister broke into a smile and offered me his outstretched hand.

'The joint has been accepted,' he said. 'You can walk again.'

For those first few seconds I felt nothing. I wasn't even aware of my own reaction, let alone Craig's and my mum's. Temporarily numbed of emotion, I thanked him for his work and pretended to listen while he talked about physiotherapy and follow-up appointments. At the end of the consultation he raised his arms and simply said, 'That's it then.'

When I got to my feet the delayed shock caught up with me, leaving me momentarily stunned. From force of habit I put my arms back in the crutches and had to muddle through freeing my arms from the stability collars that kept me connected. With no doubt about what to do next, I slid my chair back and took my first independent step in two years. As I turned back to thank Mr Isbister once more, I felt the urge to embrace him, but instead shook his hand again and left his office before I shed a tear.

As I walked down the corridor I put my hands inside my pockets. I was so accustomed to using the crutches that I didn't know what else to do with them. Ignoring the lift, I took two flights of stairs and made my way outside and across the car park. I wanted to break into a run but managed to restrain the urge. My mum and brother followed behind, both watching me in silence. When I reached the car, I threw my crutches into the boot and turned to face them.

'So that's it then.'

EPILOGUE

It goes without saying that there are lessons to be learnt from any profound experience and I often ask myself two questions, and others ask me the same ones too: 'What did you learn?' and 'How did it change you?'

Multiple near-death experiences and two years of being unable to walk must have taught me something and you'd think I would have some clearly defined answer or philosophy making sense of it all. I haven't, but I have come up with something. It involves realizing certain things about how I was before, how I am now and the ways I changed and grew as a person.

I'm certain that what had got me off the mountain were characteristics drilled into me through years of hard soldiering: physical conditioning, controlled aggression, determination, ingenuity, intuition and self-belief. In spite of everything that was chucked at me, I'd never given up because ultimately

I believed I could win through. Although they were invaluable qualities in that situation, accompanying them were less flattering characteristics: anger, stubbornness, impatience and a strong intolerance to any un-soldierly behaviour. My skill set and way of thinking were efficient, yet in so many ways I lacked dimension, creativity and emotional intelligence.

I now know that recovery doesn't run in a straight line; my rehabilitation turned out to be far more complex than simply remembering how to put one foot in front of the other. There was a whole healing process for mind, body and soul that I needed to go through in order to make a true and wholesome recovery. I had to let go of my rigid military mindset and temperament and embrace change. As my body adapted and made physical changes over the next five years, so did my way of thinking and aspects of my personality. A belated recognition of my vulnerability helped me to realize and understand that many of my drastic soldierly ways couldn't survive or help me beyond a certain point. Part of my persona had to be pushed down and patiently rebuilt.

The old military adage of 'improvise, adapt and overcome' remains as potent in my civilian life as it did throughout my military career. This change in life and temperament finds me more relaxed, content with life and at peace with myself and the world around me. I like to think some of the vital ingredients that got me off the mountain are still there, yet if I ask myself if I could still make it back today, the answer in all honesty is probably no. So, with the benefit of hindsight, I consider that many of my old characteristics served me well.

In the midst of a personal battle it's hard to see with clarity and it becomes easy to ask, 'Why did this happen to me?' When the true questions should be, 'What have I learnt from the experience that can make me a better person and what can I do to overcome my difficulties?'

As with most difficulties, those experiencing them know in their heart what they've got to do, it just takes courage to follow through.

Turning a New Corner

April 2008. I was waiting in an empty office on a military base somewhere in London. The smell of Kiwi boot polish and the conversation of soldiers in the corridor triggered memories of another time; it was funny how these small things picked up by the senses had this ability to revive larger and deeper experiences of a life I had once known. The interview with the Squadron Sergeant Major was informal, more of a chat than anything. He was neither encouraging nor discouraging, giving little away other than to say he would look at my file and I would have to pass some test marches again. I left the base with a package containing a set of joining instructions for UK Special Forces. I walked to nearby Primrose Hill Park where I had done so much of my training and found a bench in a quiet space away from other people. I sat down and tore open the top of the brown envelope and held the papers tightly in my hand. These pages were more than just routine paper work, filling them out was my gateway to a world of adventure, risk and a way of life I had known years before. All I had to do was put pen to paper to take the first step back into old territory. It felt as significant as the day I had stepped into the army career's office ten years earlier, wanting to become a paratrooper.

I rummaged inside my rucksack in search of a black biro, but instead pulled out a cigarette lighter. It was an old fake Zippo from Lithuania which I'd bought because of the red star and my birth year etched on the front. About to continue my search for a pen, I was hit by an urge to do something else. Still with the lighter in my hand, I looked at the papers sitting next to me on the bench. I wouldn't need a pen after all.

Puerto de Lizarraga, Basque Country, Spain

Summer 2009. Just under thirty minutes into the climb we approached the last hairpin bend. I switched down a gear and free-wheeled the switchback in a wide manoeuvre before leaving the saddle. The gradient kicked up and the rider in the orange jersey put the hammer down. My heart and lungs were already screaming at me and the lactic acid was turning my legs to jelly. I gripped the break hoods and pushed down on the pedals as hard as I could physically manage. His back wheel and my front were now half a wheel's distance apart. Midway up the final straight I heard the clank of a gear change, he'd clicked down onto a smaller cog and forced up the pace, making me suffer even more. I followed desperately, thinking my lungs would burst if I sustained this effort for a second longer.

Dropping back into the saddle I gripped the handlebars in the climbing position and tried to follow his ferocious pace. It was then I noticed my wrists, they were thin, bony and golden brown in colour; the black hairs had been soaked down with sweat and looked as though they had been covered in oil. As the baking hot sun beat down on me, sweat poured from my forehead, over the bridge of my nose and into my eyes. In an instant I snapped back into reality and with it the sensation of burning legs and overstretched lungs returned. My body was begging me to stop; it wasn't possible to take in any more oxygen, nor could my heart beat any faster.

With 200 metres to go the gradient dropped slightly, the gear moved down again and the speed went up. The two bikes quickly came clear of the trees and out of the protection of their shade. The open space allowed me to see the road far below snaking down the mountain in a series of wildly twisting bends until it disappeared beneath the layers of cloud that we were now riding high above.

'Keep on his wheel . . . metres to go . . .' I pleaded to my legs in desperation to hang on.

After 50 agonising metres I hit the top a few bike lengths behind the rider in orange. For a few seconds I couldn't speak and rested my head and hands on the handlebars, fighting to regain my breath. I looked up and shook my head in acknowledgement at his extraordinary climbing ability. Hardly out of breath, he casually took a sip of water from his bottle and smiled at me.

'You're a good rider,' he said.

'Not a bad compliment from a Tour de France cyclist,' I thought.

It was downhill all the way back to the village so I took a minute to take in the spectacular views across the valley and rerun the glory of the ascent through my mind. There was something about being up there that allowed my thoughts to come clearly, and in these moments, I was really able to grasp the enormity of everything I had been through and to fully appreciate the strength of my recovery. There was a lot more behind my journey to the top than pedal strokes, no matter how hard they'd been. As I sat astride my bike with the world beneath me, I felt an overwhelming sense of freedom and pride at what had passed. This ride up the mountain was a victory salute to myself.

GLOSSARY

basha: versatile shelter, sleeping bag cover or emergency carrying sheet. 'To basha up' is to make shelter and rest

Bergen: army issue backpack named after the Norwegian city of the same name

Bic: cheap brand of plastic lighter

bivi: waterproof outer lining for a sleeping bag. 'To bivi up' see 'to basha up'

bungee: elasticized cord with hooked ends usually used to secure a poncho/basha

canoe sack: re-sealable waterproof plastic bag used as a flotation device as well as for dry storage of clothing

casevac: casualty evacuation

click: one kilometre

cornice: a mass of snow and ice projecting over a mountain ridge, usually shaped by the wind into a bulging wave-like shape

crag: a steep rugged rock or peak

crampons: spiked metal platforms strapped onto boots for climbing on snow and ice

DPM: disruptive purpose/pattern material, i.e. camouflage

GPS: Global Positioning System

jack: to give up or throw in the towel, usually derogatory

Leatherman: US made multi-tool device, similar to a Swiss army knife but with the invaluable addition of pliers

lei: old Romanian currency in circulation at time of events described

LUP: British army acronym for 'laying-up position' used here to mean secure a place to rest and administrate. In military parlance a lying-up position is the term for a rallying point, forward of the Forward Operations Base (FOB). This could be a smaller base of operation where a patrol would hide while conducting missions, a hasty spot chosen for a quick rest or a place to meet in the event of enemy attack

mils: unit of measure on a compass, used mainly by militaries in artillery, tank and mortar gunnery. 17.78 mils equal $1°$. Compass use of mils typically rounds 6283 to 6400 for simplicity

NAAFI: Navy, Army, Air Force Institute

Observation Post: an observation post, temporary or fixed, is a position from which soldiers can watch enemy movements, to warn of approaching soldiers, or to direct artillery fire. In strict military terminology, an observation post is any pre-selected position from which observations are to be made

Para(s): Parachute Regiment

para cord: high strength, multi-use cord typically used for parachutes

RV: rendezvous, checkpoint or meeting place

scree: a mass of small loose stones that form or cover a slope on a mountain

Selection: physical testing procedure undertaken by volunteers for UK Special Forces

shelled: punishment; carrying of a deactivated, lead-filled artillery shell

Silva: Swedish brand of compass typically issued to British soldiers

spindrift: as far as snow goes, is defined as fine-grained snow being carried by wind or by falling. In practice it is usually used to describe the frequent spray of snow that falls down steep slopes, gullies and faces

Telemark: backcountry skis with a single free-heel mode allowing for both uphill travel and downhill skiing. Named after region of origin in Norway

thrashed: military term used to describe aggressive and unrelenting punishment in the form of physical exercises

UHF: Ultra High Frequency, as in radio/communication device

webbing: belt and shoulder rigged utility pouches typically holding ammunition, water bottles, emergency rations and other essential items dictated by military standard operating procedure

wet and dry routine: the wearing of wet clothes when active and dry clothing while at rest

Zippo: US-made metal lighter

ACKNOWLEDGEMENTS

This book is dedicated to my parents, brothers and sister who were always there for me in the darkest moments. Without the thought of them I would never have made it off the mountain and without their unrelenting love, patience and support I would never have got through everything that followed. Thanks for standing by me and patiently accepting my decision to continue climbing, racing my bike in spite of so many crashes, and all the talk of rejoining Special Forces

Thank you to the surgeons, doctors and nurses of Brasov city hospital who kept me alive. Words can never express a fraction of their true sentiment for a debt I can never repay.

Thank you to Dr Jontschew for telling it like it was and giving me hope. The physical condition I enjoy today began with our lucky encounter on the streets of Manchester. Thank you to Professor Elder for putting my stomach back together, even though you claimed to be nothing more than a simple plumber. Thank you to Mr Isbister for your enthusiasm,

287

positive outlook and fixing my hip, a job that not all were up to or willing to take on.

I'm not one to keep heroes but throughout my ordeal I have encountered many great people and experienced numerous humbling and inspiring acts that moved and impacted me profoundly. Thank you to Mum and Dad for your incredible bedside vigil in Romania, to my brother Mick for his amazing trip to Munich with my X-rays, to Craig for getting on the bike with me from the beginning and training the hard way, to my sister Laura for nursing me, to Mick Boulton for showing me how it's done and refusing to accept a quiet and inactive life. To Justin Rielly, Nick Wildman, Wes Richards, Del Yarr, Jim McCoy and Dan Norman for your friendship and absolute refusal to accept I would never walk again. The brief time I served with you all was a great honor and amongst the most memorable and enjoyable of my life. Thanks to Peter O'Donoghue and Alex Poli, wingmen as good as any to be found in my former units.

Thank you to my dear friends from Manchester University and my home county of Shropshire for your support and hospital visits, your friendship, company and letters were every bit as invaluable as the medical treatment I received. Thanks to Sue Waring from the History Department, continuing with my studies meant everything to me. Post accident, new friendships have emerged that have had an invaluable effect on my

ACKNOWLEDGEMENTS

recovery and outlook on life. Thank you to Jason Williams, George Vlase, my wife Linda De Caterina and our daughter Dharma.

My story has taken too many years to write and without the belief, encouragement and contribution of various people it would probably remain unknown. Nobody has worked harder on it than Mick Jones and my wife Linda, whose indefatigable patience and English put me to shame. Thank you to Rich O'Regan for your thoughtful input and incredible efforts to get my manuscript into the hands of someone who counted. Thanks also to Peter O'Donoghue for both your belief that I had a story worth telling and for your brilliant edit and proofread. Thanks to Josh Ireland at Quercus for taking the project on and for your professional contribution to the work.